ENDORSEMENTS

Chris Henderson is a winsome follower of Jesus. Her positive, cheerful spirit is contagious. Her faith has been tested but never broken. Visit with Chris for even a few minutes and you will be talking about Jesus and His love. I am glad she has chosen to share her rich faith with us in written form. All who read her poetry and prose will be rewarded. You will want to share her thoughts with your friends. – Walter Albritton,

Pastor of Congregational Care
Saint James United Methodist Church
9045 Vaughn Rd
Montgomery, AL 36117

I have had the humble privilege to know Chris for many years, not only as her friend, but also as one of her pastors. It has been a great joy to watch the Lord do a mighty and beautiful work in every area of her life. Her desire to know Him and honor Him has been evident as she has journeyed through various seasons.

    I have seen her unwavering faith and commitment to Jesus Christ that has enabled her to walk through various challenges with an abundance of grace, hope, joy and love. As you read this book, I know you will be blessed as she shares her deepest heart with you. I know her desire is for God to use her writings to encourage, comfort, and challenge you to intimately know the King of Kings and Lord of Lords as she does.

Janeese Spencer
Saint James United Methodist Church
Teaching Pastor

I have the distinctive pleasure of knowing Chris Henderson for several years and have benefited from her presence and participation in the Shepherds of the Cross class. Chris loves her family as only a mother truly can. We have shared common bonds of challenges in our families and have prayed for one another on many occasions. It takes courage and it takes love to unveil oneself and let others see into the very depth of one's soul. Chris has opened her heart and her soul to those who have the privilege to read this book. She has truly gotten to "the heart of the matter" and in doing so has given me a resounding "wake-up call." Thank you, Chris. You are truly blessed to be a blessing.

Bob Alred, June 15, 2007

The Heart of the Matter

Focusing On The Will Of God

Christianne Ashton Henderson

The Heart of the Matter

Copyright © 2022 by Christianne Ashton Henderson. All rights reserved.

No part of this publication may be reproduced, stored in a retrieval system or transmitted in any way by any means, electronic, mechanical, photocopy, recording or otherwise without the prior permission of the author except as provided by USA copyright law.

The opinions expressed by the author are not necessarily those of URLink Print and Media.

1603 Capitol Ave., Suite 310 Cheyenne, Wyoming USA 82001
1-888-980-6523 | admin@urlinkpublishing.com

URLink Print and Media is committed to excellence in the publishing industry.

Book design copyright © 2022 by URLink Print and Media. All rights reserved.

Published in the United States of America

Library of Congress Control Number: 2022912544
ISBN 978-1-68486-222-1 (Paperback)
ISBN 978-1-68486-223-8 (Digital)

24.05.22

CONTENTS

Preface..7
Chapter 1: Focusing on Our Hearts...............................11
Chapter 2: Focusing on Our Pains.................................16
Chapter 3: Focusing on Prayer and God's Answer.......22
Chapter 4: Focusing on God's Mercy.............................30
Chapter 5: Focusing on God's Healing..........................33
Chapter 6: Focusing on Our Walk with Jesus...............37
Chapter 7: Focusing on Our Growth in the Lord........44
Chapter 8: Focusing on Our Problems..........................49
Chapter 9: Focusing on Our Recovery..........................52
Chapter 10: Focusing on God's Will in Our Lives........55
Chapter 11: Focusing on Our Gifts.................................61
Chapter 12: Focusing on Commitment 65

Part B: The Heart of the Matter 69
Chapter 13: Increasing Our Intimate Relationship with Jesus 71
Chapter 14: Focusing on Our Work in the World.......75
Chapter 15: Focusing on Our Health.............................80
Chapter 16: Focusing on Our Families..........................84
Chapter 17: Focusing on Our Friends and Neighbors.................88
Chapter 18: Focusing on His Service 92
Chapter 19: Focusing on Our Personal Commitments.................96
Chapter 20: The Heart of the Matter... Focusing on the Will of God..102

PREFACE

"And we know that in all things God works for the good of those who love Him, who have been called according to His purpose."

(Romans 8:28)

God has been speaking directly to me for a number of years; sometimes I listened, sometimes I did not. For most of my life I have been a "practicing" Christian, attending church, even following God's lead in all aspects of my life, I thought. But many times God has had to give me a serious "wake-up call" to get my attention to focus on His will. This book tells my story and it could be your story—the story of what can happen to us in our lives, things that will change our lives, destroy them or improve them—depending on God's will and our focus on His will. Imagine an unexpected heart attack improving your life!

Jesus can use distress and disasters to improve our lives and intensify our relationships with Him. Sometimes we are very surprised by things that happen to us. We may be overwhelmed, feel defeated or depressed by the events and tragedies that we face, or we can trust the Lord to use these tragedies and unexpected sorrows that we face in our lives our lives on earth and our lives with Him – in positive ways. Think about what happened to Jesus on the cross and how He responded to the pain and agony. Jesus suffered for us and obeyed His father's will, even in the most tragic time of His life. As He prayed in Gethsemane before His crucifixion, He did not give up, but prayed for God's will to be done, "My father, if it is possible, may this cup be taken from me. Yet not as I will, but as You will" (Matthew 26:39). Jesus came closer to His Father as He prayed in the garden. We often become distracted by anger or envy, by our individual successes or failures or by the overcrowding of our lives and we do not come closer to our Father. Can we allow God's will to be in our lives as Jesus did?

Psalm 73:21-22 described me at this moment of my life that changed me and changed my lifestyle, "When my heart was grieved and my spirit embittered, I was senseless and ignorant; I was a brute beast before You." I now ask myself, "How long was I looking to Jesus for the source of my spiritual life?" Billy Graham describes what I experienced in "The Brightness of God's Love" in his book, Hope for Each Day: "Trouble will not hurt us unless it does what many of us too often allow it to do-harden us, making us sour, bitter, and skeptical. But it need not be this way. Troubles we bear trustfully can bring us a fresh vision of God and a new outlook on life—an outlook of peace and hope."

We must wait for God's will to be revealed and activated in our hearts. Waiting is difficult for most of us. We must focus on this scripture, "Wait for the Lord; be strong and take heart and wait for the Lord" (Psalm 27:14). In The Heart of the Matter, you will read about miracles delivered by God, both physical and spiritual changes of the heart. We must all focus on Him and not on ourselves, which is sometimes a hard thing to do. Remember this message in John 14:1, "Do not let your hearts be troubled. Trust in God; trust also in me." God has not promised to deliver us from all troubles, but He has promised to go with us through the troubles.

The writing of this book was clearly an inspiration from the Lord. I turned to this scripture so many times immediately after my "wake-up call" that I knew Jesus was speaking directly to me and this time I will listen. Writing is my hobby, and when Jesus wants us to use any gift that He has given us, we must be faithful. I have reread and reread this scripture in Jeremiah 30:2 for years, feeling a calling from Jesus. At last, I am going to respond to His orders in this verse: "This is what the Lord, the God of Israel, says: "Write in a book all the words I have spoken to you.""

The changes that have evolved in my life style have made it possible for me to spend time following His will and writing about my experiences and have enhanced my relationship with Jesus. Prior to this time, I rarely found time to actually sit and write or even reflect on my thoughts or His word.

> *"I waited patiently for the Lord; He turned to me and heard my cry. He lifted me out of the slimy pit, out of the mud and mire; He set my feet on a rock and gave me a firm place to stand." (Psalm 40:1-2)*

CHAPTER 1

Focusing on Our Hearts

"May He strengthen your hearts so that you will be blameless and holy in the presence of our God and Father when our Lord Jesus comes with all His holy ones. (1 Thessalonians 3:13)

Our hearts are the heart of the matter, physically and spiritually. We must have healthy hearts in order to live healthy lives and we must commit our hearts to our Father, Lord of all heaven and earth, to live eternal lives. The Bible uses the word, "heart" repeatedly to speak of our minds, souls and wills. Actually, our hearts are the vital centers of both desire and will and the wellspring of action. We must submit our wills to Him and follow Him in all we do because life is more than just being happy or successful. Proverbs 4:23-25 tells us how important our hearts are in our lives, "Above all else, guard your heart, for it is the wellspring of life. Put away perversity from your mouth; keep corrupt talk from your lips. Let your eyes look straight ahead, fix your gaze directly before you."

What happens in our lives is always connected to our hearts, whether we are with Jesus or separated from Him by our worldly actions and desires. I always remember this scripture when I think of the word "heart," "Trust in the Lord with all your heart and lean not on your own understanding; in all your ways acknowledge Him, and He will make your paths straight. Do not be wise in your own eyes;

fear the Lord and shun evil. This will bring health to your body and nourishment to your bones" (Proverbs 3:5-8).

I have read that particular scripture many times and even memorized it, something I rarely ever did. But did I really "trust in the Lord" with all my heart? I thought that I did. I "trusted" God but still tried to maintain control of my life and my problems. Of course I considered myself wise; I acknowledged the Lord for making me wise and capable of taking care of all of my needs, desires and problems. I did not, however, with my whole heart, follow this call, "Let us draw near to God with a sincere heart in full assurance of faith, having our hearts sprinkled to cleanse us from a guilty conscience and having our bodies washed with pure water" (Hebrews 10:22).

Like so many people, I believed in faith. I knew that the scriptures I read were direct messages from our Lord. In December of 2006, God gave me a very clear "wake-up" call. I may hear His word but I do not always listen. I have to be reminded by Romans 10:8-10: "'The word is near you; it is in your mouth and in your heart,' that is the word of faith we are proclaiming: That if you confess with your mouth, 'Jesus is Lord,' and believe in your heart that God raised Him from the dead you will be saved".

The Lord is near us, always, every moment of every day. We must acknowledge His presence and listen to His voice. His voice speaks "His word" to us. Yes, I believed that Jesus was raised from the dead; I believed this with all my heart. But I was not recognizing how close He was to me and I certainly was not listening.

I considered myself reasonably healthy for a sixty-five year old woman who did not ever want to acknowledge my age yet frequently used my age as an excuse to justify my concerns, failures and bitterness. At this time in my life, I was surprisingly rarely ever ill, thanking God throughout each day for taking such good care of me. I praised the Lord in prayers, listened to my favorite praise music every day and worshiped Him in all church related opportunities. I knew that our Father was caring for me so that I could assist my diabetic husband with his heart conditions and other issues. I repeated this scripture almost every day: "I will praise the Lord, who counsels me; even at night my heart instructs me" (Psalm 16:7). I also knew that Jesus had a purpose for me to do His will in my life: at home, at work and in my church. But was I focused on His purpose for me or on my purposes as I interpreted them?

This scripture has always been a focus of our church: "'For I know the plans I have for you' declares the Lord, 'plans to prosper you and not to harm you, plans to give you hope and a future.'" (Jeremiah 29:11). After studying <u>The Purpose Driven Life</u> and writing multiple poems about God's plans for me, I was confident that I was living my life according to His will. If we do not experience lack of control, we usually feel that we are focusing on His will, don't we? Yet when we do experience those moments and days of lack of control, we often blame our Father for not caring for us. This scripture comes to mind when we think about control, "The mind of sinful man is death, but the mind controlled by the Spirit is life and peace" (Romans 8:6).

My attendance at work was excellent. Infrequent absences and minimum use of my vacation days had increased my sick leave and accrued vacation days far beyond my expectations. I actually anticipated major or long-term illnesses because of working with very medically fragile children who are frequently ill and staff who often became ill and had to take leave. I prayed that God would dwell within my heart more and more so that I would be equipped to face the realities of life. Jeremiah 33:6 should be remembered as we pray about our health, "I will heal my people and will let them enjoy abundant peace and security." In spite of my prayers and feeling close to God, I was still often stressed out because of issues at work and at home. Do you have worries that cause stress or anxiety? We all do at different times in our lives

I felt that sometimes people come into our lives, leave footprints on our hearts, and we are never the same. I remember the scripture from II Timothy 2:22, "Pursue righteousness, faith, love and peace, along with those who call on the Lord out of a pure heart." But did I have a pure heart? I do not think that I could have used this scripture to describe my life, "Give me understanding and I will keep your law and obey it with all my heart" (Psalm 119:34). We need to remember this message in I Samuel 16:7, "The Lord does not look at the things man looks at. Man looks at the outward appearance, but the Lord looks at the heart."

I should have been praying Psalm 51:10, especially at this time in my life, "Create in me a pure heart, O God, and renew a steadfast spirit within me." Sometimes, opening our hearts before God can be scary. Do we really want Him to see what is in our hearts? Are we comfortable saying, "Search me, O God, and know my heart; test me and know my anxious thoughts"? (Psalm 139:23). I probably did not want God to actually see what was in my heart because of my fears and anger. Would you open your heart to God? Will you let Him see what is in your heart and on your mind?

I was aware that I was receiving daily messages from Jesus. But He often had to get my attention in a very dramatic way. At this time, He "touched" my heart and got my attention! What causes heart attacks? Medically speaking, we are probably all aware of the multiple conditions that may cause heart attacks or other heart conditions. I had been diagnosed with a very simple congenital heart defect, blood clotting problems and arrhythmia. The medicines I had been taking for over ten years, however, usually controlled these minor problems. I rarely experienced any symptoms of this condition and had been hospitalized only a few times. I never expected a heart attack at my age.

I certainly would never have anticipated the heart attack to be an answer to my prayers! We must be careful for what we pray because Jesus hears our prayers and knows our hearts. Again, we must refer to this scripture in Jeremiah, "'Then you will call upon me and come and pray to me, and I will listen to you. You will seek me and find me when you seek me with all your heart. I will be found by you,' declares the Lord and 'will bring you back from captivity'" (Jeremiah 29: 12-14). Sometimes we pray for what we want or think we want, instead of praying for God's will to be done. I frequently cried out to Jesus. I prayed specifically for needs that I had identified for myself, my family and others. I frequently repeated these words from Philippians 4:6-8:

"Do not be anxious about anything, but in everything, by prayer and petition, with thanksgiving, present your requests to God. And the peace of God, which transcends all understanding, will guard your hearts and your minds in Christ Jesus. Finally, brothers, whatever is true, whatever is noble, whatever is right, whatever is pure, whatever is lovely, whatever is admirable —if anything is excellent or praiseworthy—think about such things."

But I was anxious. I did not ask the Lord to help me understand what is "true" or "noble" or "right" or "pure" or "lovely" or "admirable." In my mind, I thought I understood. But in my heart I did not. A lot of our prayers consist of politely telling God how we think things should be. Specific prayers are desired by God but He wants us to follow His lead and make those requests to honor Him and complete His plan for us. Read Mark 10:35-44, the request of James and John. How did Jesus respond to this request? What did the other disciples think? Were James and John noble, right, pure, lovely or admirable? Are our prayers and requests sometimes far from nobility, righteousness, purity, beauty or admiration?

Even though I sometimes prayed, "Your will be done," I continued to pray for my help and specific needs as I interpreted them. It seems that control freaks like me think that we are to ask and receive but still maintain control ourselves. I definitely anticipated answers to my prayers but now I realize how extremely responsive God can be. When the pain hit my heart shortly after midnight a couple of days after Christmas, I thought that I was having a severe indigestion problem.

In my compulsive and obsessive manner, I was cleaning my house after everyone else had gone to bed, storing away things after a busy Christmas holiday. Physical pain can certainly be heartache at times. I ignored the pain for a few minutes but quickly realized that it was much more serious than indigestion or heartburn. Yes, it was heartburn but nothing like what I had ever experienced. My heart was burning because of my spirit.

> *"Even though I walk through the valley of the shadow of death, I will fear no evil, for You are with me." Psalm 23:4*

CHAPTER 2

Focusing on Our Pains

"O Lord my God, I called to you for help and you healed me."

(Psalm 30:2)

Remember how Jesus suffered on the cross? His pain washed away our sins. We cannot begin to imagine the severe pain that He experienced. Can prayer cause pain and even a heart attack? My selfish prayer did! The 2006 Christmas season was a culmination of serious problems with which my family had been dealing for many months. My husband's mother and father both resided in nursing homes and required lots of support and chores; they also needed almost daily visits and trips to meet their needs.

In addition to these family problems, my husband and I had encouraged our divorced daughter and her children to move into our home to get away from devastating situations caused by a traumatic divorce and disassociation of their family. We were trying to care for her and her family until their needs could be met and they could live independently. At this time, I should have been repeating this message from Christ to myself and to my family, especially in our times of crisis, "And surely I am with you always, to the very end of the age" (Matthew 28:20). Do we forget that He is with us because we are so overwhelmed by our lives?

The Heart of the Matter

An "empty nest" is very difficult for parents when it happens. Most of us really dread the anticipation of that sad, empty nest, worrying about our children growing up and leaving our homes. But long-term "empty nest" parents become accustomed to a quiet life with simple and complex problems handled only by the two of them. It is difficult when "birds" return to the "nest" and require space, help and support. It is equally difficult for the "bird" to become a "child" again, feeling lack of self-control and self-confidence. We turned over all of the upstairs rooms to them in an attempt to make them feel that they sort of had a "home" that was not the old nest.

It is equally important for the "bird" returning to the empty nest to rely on God's will and His blessings: "Many are the plans in a man's heart, but it is the Father's purpose that prevails," (Proverbs 19:21). If the Father's purpose does not prevail in that "bird's" life, it is often difficult for us to meet the needs and desires of the "bird." These circumstances produced multiple incidents and concerns: financial, social, emotional, physical and spiritual. Lack of having a "real" home, missing their pets and their friends and having no "normal" mother/father relationships or "happy" holidays can cause serious trauma for teenagers. Their frustrations and disappointments are frequently manifested in overall anger, depression, illnesses and lack of cooperation. We must always remember that God's joy and peace neutralize sin's poison and promote emotional and physical health. But my family ignored His joy and peace because of our disappointments and frustrations.

The teens sometimes got upset with their mother. Her serious problems produced by abuse, a very devastating divorce, lack of positive self-concept because of the treatment she had received in her life and having to become a "child" again interfered with her entire life. She was overcome by depression and anxiety, frequently causing her to be very sick and need medication.

During these stressful times, I found myself praying every day, almost every minute of every day! I recited Matthew 21:22 in my mind at all times, "If you believe, you will receive whatever you ask for in prayer." I felt that I was rooting my life in prayer, depending on the Lord. But I should have thought of this message:

> "And when you pray, do not keep on babbling like pagans, for they think they will be heard because of their many words. Do not be like them, for your Father knows what you need before you ask Him." (Matthew 6:7-8)

And, I should have prayed a prayer of surrender, "Father, I give you my life. Please fill me now and use me in whatever way You want." Instead, I was probably repeatedly crying out, "...My God, my God, why have you forsaken me?" (Matthew 27:46). We often doubt one of God's promises because it seems so long in coming to fulfillment. Let us remember what David said in Psalm 16:8, "I have set the Lord always before me. Because He is at my right hand, I will not be shaken." Look at your right hand. Do you feel God's presence in your life, His closeness to you? Or do you feel like you are shaking?

Christmas should be a happy time, a time to celebrate the birth of our savior. My husband and I had purchased several gifts for everyone but major concerns were expressed by our daughter immediately before Christmas Eve. The teens were concerned about having a good Christmas and we feared that we had not prepared for Santa's usual Christmas. Under pressure and caring for the children, we "played Santa," despite our age and our ongoing stresses in many aspects of our lives

Supporting two families when one parent is retired is difficult. The costs of Christmas and frequent costs of medical treatment and medicines for the family were becoming quite oppressive to my husband and me. We were trying to provide the best home and especially the best Christmas that we could for our entire family, worrying more about their needs than about our budget. I remembered another Psalm of David, "O Lord, I call to you; come quickly to me. Hear my voice when I call to You. May my prayer be set before You like incense; may the lifting up of my hands be like the evening sacrifice" (Psalm 141:1-2). I really wanted to see a miracle to make the situation more bearable for our children and grandchildren. I was praying to the Lord to "come quickly to me," and my family.

The Heart of the Matter

In addition to our family stresses, I had been experiencing serious management problems in my position as a principal of a school for severely disabled students and executive director of a non-profit organization. Both jobs mesh but often create extreme multi-tasking and major problems related to both aspects of the position. On the job, stress had increased daily during the two months before Christmas. I was dealing with situations that were practically unimaginable. I had spent more time behind closed doors trying to resolve problems during those months than during the entire last three years. Making the job even more difficult was my problem of not delegating duties in a logical and practical manner, preferring to do things myself, the way I wanted them done.

But with all the stress in my life, I had begun to see the need to share responsibilities and improve this aspect of my position. I was "getting there," but I actually had a long way to go. We frequently find it easier to "handle" our problems ourselves than to "hand" them to those who can help us, don't we?

During this stressful time in my life, I usually awoke with worry every morning after tossing and turning with concerns on my mind throughout the night. Even after praying and repeatedly thinking of these verses in Matthew 11:28-30, I continued to toss and turn, "Come to me, all you who are weary and burdened, and I will give you rest. Take my yoke upon you and learn from me, for I am gentle and humble in heart, and you will find rest for your souls. For my yoke is easy and my burden is light." I have been repeating this message from Jesus for most of my life. It is actually one of the first scriptures that I ever memorized

During these nights of worry and little sleep, I literally dreamed about the school, frequently experiencing what most people would call nightmares, then awakening multiple times during the nights and the next mornings without having experienced any rest or peace. This scripture from Psalm 6:6-7 very clearly describes my frustration at this time, "I am worn out from groaning; all night long I flood my bed with weeping and drench my couch with tears. My eyes grow weak with sorrow." Actually, I should have referred to this scripture and taken it into my heart; "Be at rest once more, O my soul, for the Lord has been good to you" (Psalm 116:7)

In the hard-driving culture in which we reside today, we tend to value others and ourselves on the basis of what we produce. I certainly became very frustrated if I could not see excellent completion of duties and projects. Power and self-reliance are two of our generation's most valued and dangerous characteristics. Our tough lives can beat us up! We forget that this is the time to run to the Lord, not away from the Lord. Rest becomes even more essential in our busy world. In my mind, I knew that I needed to find time for real rest, especially during bedtime hours. I did not, however, place my cares and concerns in God's capable hands, taking time to enjoy praying or playing in my life! And I was not enjoying my most precious relationship—the relationship with our Lord, the Holy Spirit and Jesus. We must remember that we should not be distracted by the cataclysmic events going on around us as they create a gap between Jesus and us.

I believe that I was the prime example of Proverbs 17:22, "A cheerful heart is good medicine, but a crushed spirit dries up the bones." I was deeply concerned about how to handle all of my problems. I prayed; I said that I had turned it all over to the Lord, yet I still worried. I did not attend to this quotation from Ralph Waldo Emerson, "What lies behind us and what lies before us are tiny matters compared to what lies in us." I also should have remembered the scripture from James 4:8, "Come near to God and He will come near to you. Wash your hands, you sinners, and purify your hearts, you double-minded."

I certainly was double minded. I prayed to our Father all day, everyday—in the car, in meetings, during meals and at other times. But I had become so busy and stressed out that it was unusual for me to arise early enough to have my designated quiet time with the Lord. I gave up reading my Bible every day and was no longer journaling at all. But I continued my repetitious prayers, saying, "I'm turning it over to you, Lord." I think of the words from Ephesians 1:18 as I look back on this time, "I pray also that the eyes of your heart may be enlightened in order that you may know the hope to which He has called you." Although I read and heard the word, even changing the words to personalize His message, (I pray that the eyes of my heart may be enlightened in order that I may know the hope to which He has called me), hope was obviously not part of my heart; I was not depending on Jesus with all my heart. My heart was not enlightened.

> *"Our help is in the name of the Lord, the maker of heaven and earth." (Psalm 124:8)*

CHAPTER 3

Focusing on Prayer and God's Answer

"Be still before the Lord and wait patiently for Him; do not fret when men succeed in their ways, when they carry out their wicked schemes." (Psalm 37:7)

Christmas, as described in Chapter 2, was a difficult time, although joy and happiness overrode the difficulties. However, a major confrontation between two family members occurred after dinner on the evening of Christmas Day. The conflict went on for hours and was very emotionally draining to me. I had overheard the beginning of the argument and eventually was involved in trying to resolve the problem. I tried to use my counseling talents to help them work out the problem. Further counseling with the two of them resulted in a commitment to seek outside help. Nevertheless, anger and despair were present the rest of the evening. If our hearts are cluttered, resistant, hardened, we are usually closed to God and others who care for us rather than close to them.

When I shared the details of the incident with my husband, we both felt disappointed and helpless. We prayed together that night and the next night. We shared our faith from Matthew 7:7-8, "Ask and it will be given to you; seek and you will find; knock and the door will be opened to you. For everyone who asks receives; he who seeks finds; and to him who knocks, the door will be opened." I prayed this very positive prayer in a very negative way, not really believing that any door would be opened for us at all; I think that I envisioned a lost key. I also could have listened to God's word and quit worrying so much, "So then, banish anxiety from your heart and cast off the troubles of your body..." (Ecclesiastes 11:10).

Depression, negativity, sadness, worry and frustration were prominent in all aspects of our lives at this point. My husband and I still could not agree on solutions and possible plans to resolve our problems and improve all of our relationships. I was very frustrated. I felt so depressed. I continued to pray and talk with Jesus almost every other breath. Still, no solutions or possible moves came to us. The second night after Christmas, I was totally as low as I had ever been. I said that I was at the bottom of my rope (I forgot to tell myself to tie a knot in it and hang on!). Having recently read two books about heaven as a result of inspirational sermons and lessons at my church, <u>Ninety Minutes in Heaven</u> and <u>Heaven is So Real,</u> I thought about how wonderful heaven will be—no problems, no confrontations—just beauty, peace and joy.

As I lay in bed, trying to relax, I began to pray for peace for my family. I specifically told Jesus that I was going to turn my family problems over to Him. But suddenly, I sat up in the bed and began to pray: "Lord, please bring me home. I know how wonderful heaven is and I would prefer to be there with You rather than having to live like this on earth. Please, Lord," I prayed, "bring me home, remove me from this frustrating world and let me go to heaven." I prayed very seriously, crying as I cried out to Jesus to please release me from the pains of my life

My husband awoke and I told him, in tears, what I had just prayed. This information caused stress and sadness for him—it was very obvious. He said that he was extremely unhappy that I had felt this desire and that I would ask for such a solution. I apologized to him but told him that I was very serious. "I cannot live like this any more," I said. "I feel totally helpless." I cried and cried, tossing and turning. How many times in our lives do even believers reach this point?

I thought I was listening to Jesus, but actually I was crying so hard and crying out so loudly that I really was not listening at all. My pain was the focus of my prayers. I should have realized that when our voices are so loud, we cannot hear His whisper or even His vibrant voice. I should have listened to what Peter wrote, "Cast all your anxiety on Him because He cares for you" (1 Peter 5:7). When we are so anxious, we don't even think about casting our anxiety on Him, do we?

The next day was busy and a fun time as all of the girls in our family shopped, toured the city and fellowshipped with each other. During a quiet moment that day, I experienced a strange thought about Christmas. I said to myself that I was glad that all of the family had been together for this last time. When I recognized the word, "last" and realized the seriousness of my thought, I felt taken aback. I knew that I was physically tired and emotionally drained because of the duties of hosting Christmas Eve and Christmas Day. I was exhausted, also, because my husband had developed a serious case of gout and we had had to go to the ER and his doctor's office for the past three days to try to help him overcome the pain and swelling.

Everyone had gone to bed fairly late on the evening of my "wake-up call," but as a "night owl," I was still excited to have some time alone without any interruptions or confrontations. I have always enjoyed my time alone whether I am praying, reading the Bible, working on paperwork or cleaning. Being a "night owl," I began to clean up the great room and kitchen. I cleaned the refrigerator and pantry, and then began storing holiday items that we would no longer need. At about midnight, I started vacuuming and dusting, hoping to have the room in perfect order before going to bed (OCD: obsessive, compulsive disorder seems to be one of my characteristics). I knew that I could not go to bed until it was completed. Shortly after midnight, I ate a little snack and drank some of my favorite Diet Coke, looking for more energy to help me finish my tasks.

After eating my cheese and crackers, I reached for the vacuum cleaner. I suddenly felt tightness and stifling pain in my chest. I thought, "Oh, no. Not more indigestion and reflux problems," chastising myself for snacking so late, especially for eating the pepper jelly with cheese that I had just consumed. Almost immediately, the pain increased. If a doctor or nurse had asked me at what level, from one to ten, I would measure the pain, I would have said twenty. I had never, in my entire life, ever experienced that kind of pain. I envisioned a huge elephant standing on my chest, jumping up and down. I suddenly remembered reading a poster in the emergency room that very week with my husband about heart attack symptoms for women and recognized the descriptions of the pain. When one crisis arises in our lives, we frequently experience multiple problems and disruptions, don't we?

I immediately fell to my knees beside the ottoman. My first thought, as I knelt, was about the prayer I had prayed the previous evening. I cried out, "Lord, I am so sorry. I know that what happens to me is Your will, not my will. I am sorry that I asked You to do something that was not initiated by You. It is in Your hands, Lord. I know now that I want only to do Your will." As the pain continued to increase, I cried and prayed, asking for forgiveness for not depending on Jesus. I confessed that I had not trusted in Him but had been trying to handle my problems my way. I acknowledged that Heaven would be a lovely place to go, but now I wanted to go only according to His timing and His will. It was not my call. Then I remembered that all things come to us from God's fatherly hand, not by chance.

At once, I remembered the verse from Philippians 4:19, "And my God will meet all your needs according to His glorious riches in Christ Jesus." I understood that this pain was not a coincidence. But I felt that the Lord had heard me and was responding to my prayer. I was still crying tears of shame. This scripture came to my mind immediately, "For it is God who works in you to will and to act according to His good purpose" (Philippians 2:13). I realized that it is not all about me, but all about Him.

After praying and crying, my compulsive personality kicked in again and I tried to continue to dust the tables in the great room. The pain began to spread to my neck, upper back, back of my head and my arms. It was definitely the reemphasis of the "wake-up call." I was very worried but I remembered what Matthew had written in 6:27, "Who of you by worrying can add a single hour to his life?" I also thought about a statement I had recently read: "It's easy to remember God when we're in trouble and forget about God's presence in ordinary times." God was helping me reach out to Him. It was definitely a "wake-up call"! Hebrews 4:7 immediately came to my mind, "Today, if you hear His voice, do not harden your hearts."

My daughter had awakened and appeared in the kitchen, seeing me sitting on the floor in the great room. I asked her to get some nitroglycerine pills from her dad. I actually had my own bottle of pills but did not know where I had put them. My husband came into the room with the pills in his hand. He was in shock, obviously aware that this was a genuine heart attack. He told my daughters to call the paramedics. At any other time, I would have protested and rejected such a serious solution. I did not refuse any help! I actually used three of the pills, placing them under my tongue, as prescribed. The pain continued. Sometimes we miss warnings we should have heeded. We see them only after the fact, unfortunately, not so clearly beforehand. We probably cry out, "How long, O Lord, must I call for help, but you do not listen?" (Habakkuk 1:2)

I clearly saw this warning from my Father. I remembered what Jesus had said to the disciples when they were in the boat after the storm, "Why are you so afraid? Do you still have no faith?" (Mark 4:40). My faith returned. I was in extreme pain but I felt at peace. Two paramedics arrived and began procedures and tests. At first it appeared that they were uncertain that I was having a heart attack. Very, soon, however, they suggested requesting an ambulance to take me to the hospital, confirming the diagnosis of a heart attack.

I continued to cry and whispered to my husband about my prayer and God's answer to prayer. He assured me that my Father was taking care of me. I also continued to pray, this time actually turning it over to my Father and hearing these words in my heart, "Do not be afraid or discouraged because of this vast army. For the battle is not yours, but God's" (II Chronicles 20: 15). I knew that this problem was for my benefit. Rising above a circumstance will heal us in many ways, physically and spiritually. Pain can actually be an advantage. Hezekiah gave thanks for the difficulties he faced in Isaiah 38:17, "Surely it was for my benefit that I suffered such anguish. In

Your love You kept me from the pit of destruction; You have put all my sins behind Your back." Hezekiah continued to praise our father, "The Lord will save me, and we will sing with stringed instruments all the days of our lives in the temple of the Lord" (Isaiah 38:20). Do we praise Him for all of our blessings? Do we ever praise Him when we face trials and tribulations?

Problems that we face can strengthen us. Still in pain but confident that whatever happened would be the Lord's will and His decision would be to my benefit, I arrived at the emergency room. I do not remember leaving the ambulance but I can still recall the room in which I was placed and the large number of nurses and doctors who surrounded me. They confirmed that a heart attack was definitely happening. I cried and told my husband that I had confessed to Jesus that I was sorry for trying to control my world and not obeying His calling and His will. I recalled having read a sentence in my study Bible that reminds us that when life's burdens are too heavy to bear, the Lord will lift our weary souls. If God chose to take me home or if He chose to let my life continue, I would be at peace.

I did not get upset when I heard someone ask my husband to sign a form approving a heart catheterization. I did not even lose it when another form was presented to him to agree to open heart surgery if the test indicated a need. I knew that I was going to be healed in one way or another. I could feel it in my heart the one in my chest and the spiritual one. I could feel His presence in the room. I could feel His hand on me when a doctor arrived and I was taken to a room for the procedure. Remembering the story of Asa in II Chronicles 16:12, where we are told to call on God as well as physicians, I felt confident.

Some people might think it is weird to feel at peace and be happy under these circumstances, but remember what James wrote, "Consider it pure joy, my brothers, whenever you face trials of many kinds, because you know that the testing of your faith develops perseverance" (James 1:2-3). Sometimes, it takes many trials and tribulations for God to get our attention. Do we think of those times as "pure joy?" We should recognize that joy can come from perseverance and faith.

I always knew that God answers prayers. Frequently, however, I did not always see His answers or even try to envision them. Now, I recall this prayer of David, "In my distress I called to the Lord; I cried to my God for help. From His temple He heard my voice; my cry came before Him, into His ears" (Psalm 18:6). I shall always continue to repeat this prayer and keep it in my heart, although I cannot recall the origin of these words: "Hear my prayer, O Lord, let my cry for help come to you. Do not hide Your face from me when I am in distress. Turn Your ear to me; when I call, answer me quickly, according to Your will." But more importantly, I will remember that God is always with me and I will continue my ongoing daily prayers in all aspects of my life, knowing that God hears my whispers and my cries. He knows my heart. I will not be afraid, I will believe. We do not have to reach this point of desperation. God always hears our prayers! He does not hide His face from us or turn His ears away. We simply must maintain an intimate relationship with Him and know that He hears our prayers and that His timing is perfect.

Attending to His voice and His answers, however, requires our efforts. We are so unaccustomed to listening that we often let God's messages go unnoticed. Or we hear God speaking to us but we don't let the words take root in our inner beings. We often let problems and pleasures overshadow His word. Even more vital is this message from James to help us focus on our messages from God, "Do not merely listen to the word, and so deceive yourselves. Do what it says" (James 1:22). God's word is our strength. We should commit to know His word and follow His word. Let's read Psalm 119:11 to remind us of this need, "I have hidden Your word in my heart that I might not sin against You."

Let us pray for God's will to be done in our lives, remembering what Paul wrote in I Corinthians 10:23-24, "Everything is permissible'—but not everything is beneficial. 'Everything is permissible'—but not everything is constructive. Nobody should seek his own good, but the good of others." I was only thinking of myself, certainly not behaving in a constructive way. From now on,

"I wait for the Lord, my soul waits, and in His word I put my hope" (Psalm 130:5).

> *"I lift up my eyes to the hills---where does my help come from? My help comes from the lord, the maker of heaven and earth" (Psalm 121:1-2)*

CHAPTER 4

Focusing on God's Mercy

"Mercy triumphs over judgment!" (James 2:13)

God's great mercy and love wash down over us when we are afraid or in need. What is it that we fear? Many people sincerely believe in heaven but still fear death. Many of us fear leaving our families and friends to live our eternal lives with Jesus. We also greatly fear judgment and discipline in all aspect of our lives. We continue to worry about the issues over which we feel we have no control, or more importantly, we worry about the issues that we think we must control ourselves, regardless of how out of control those issues are. We often forget that our Father is a shepherd and we are the sheep. He casts His mercy upon us as deeply as the shepherd watches and cares for the flock, "He tends His flock like a shepherd: He gathers the lambs in His arms and carries them close to His heart; He gently leads those that have young" (Isaiah 40:11).

God very clearly cast His mercy upon me in my home and in the hospital. He was caring for me even when I did not seem to care about following His will. I had not followed God's requirements. I tried to control my life and all of the problems that I faced in my life. I should have focused on Jesus twenty-four/seven instead of being distracted by the seemingly overwhelming events going on around me. God uses mercy and discipline to help us return to Him and focus on His word, not our words. Most of us do not like to be disciplined, but we must remember,

> *"No discipline seems pleasant at the time, but painful. Later on, however, it produces a harvest of righteousness and peace for those who have been trained by it"* (Hebrews 12:11).

I knew that I had not been faithful to Jesus. I knew that I should never have asked Him to do such a big thing in my life if it was not His call. My prayers, however, were heard during this traumatic trial in my life. God uses challenges, tragedies, diseases and other difficulties to strengthen and purify us. We must turn to Him in our tragedies: "Let us then approach the throne of grace with confidence, so that we may receive mercy and find grace to help us in our time of need" (Hebrews 4:16).

And that is what I did! I prayed to God with confidence that I wanted His mercy and assured Him that I was at peace with His next step in my life. The pain in my physical heart was intense, but there was no longer pain in my spiritual heart. I realized that once again, all things come to us not by chance but from our Father's hand. I knew that the Lord would provide the correct solution for my problems. This knowledge is confirmed by Philippians 4:19, "And my God will meet all your needs according to His glorious riches in Christ Jesus."

A heart attack was for my benefit! Is that not amazing? God answered my prayer with an unanticipated response. After the catheterization, I was elated, but not surprised, to hear that my heart attack had been real but that the blood clot which obviously caused it had dissolved and no damage was present in my heart and no surgery was needed. From that moment, early in my hospitalization, I realized that my life was being changed. I will remain on earth but I am going to live my life according to God's will. It is all about Him, not about me. I will surrender my heart to Him. My heart is His heart! He spoke to me directly, "For through me your days will be many, and years will be added to your life" (Proverbs 9:11). Another amazing scripture came to mind as I pondered the attack and the results:

> *"How much more, then, will the blood of Christ, who through the eternal Spirit offered Himself unblemished to God, cleanse our consciences from acts that lead to death, so that we may serve the living God!" (Hebrews 9:14).*

I remembered that in a Bible study we had talked about how God is present whether we think we need Him or not. His presence is not always dramatic; He is with us in natural events, looking over us as our shepherd. It is true God is with us. From this moment forward, I committed to seek Him in every aspect of my life; my decision was reiterated by this scripture, "So do not fear, for I am with you; do not be dismayed, for I am your God. I will strengthen you and help you; I will uphold you with my righteous right hand" (Isaiah 41:10). We must focus always on the mercy of our Father.

God is gracious! Always remember, "the wisdom that comes from heaven is first of all pure; then peace-loving, considerate, submissive, full of mercy and good fruit, impartial and sincere" (James 3:17). In my mind, I continued to sing one of my favorite praise song verses, "All my days, I will sing this song of gladness, I will praise the fountain of delight, for in my helplessness you heard my cry, and waves of mercy poured down on my life." As stated in this song, Jesus is a beautiful savior and a wonderful counselor!

"The Lord will keep you from all harm-He will watch over your life." (Psalm 121:7)

CHAPTER 5

Focusing on God's Healing

"The Lord is a refuge for the oppressed, a stronghold in times of trouble." (Psalm 9:9)

From the moment I had prayed the prayer of forgiveness, I was at peace. Yes, I continued to cry because I was sorry about trying to control God. Yes, I continued to cry because I had hurt my family and caused them so much concern. Yes, I continued to cry tears of happiness because I had heard Jesus speak to me, "Change your life, daughter; don't give up your life. I still have a purpose for you in this world." Remember that God is one "who is able to do immeasurably more than all we ask or imagine, according to His power that is at work within us" (Ephesians 3:20).

I know that what I have read in Philippians 4:13 is critical for us to remember, "I can do everything through Him who gives me strength." Remember also, that Jesus rescues, comforts, confronts and challenges us in our lives. We must learn to rely on His miraculous power for He will give us strength in our times of need. With His miraculous power, I awoke in the cardiovascular ICU, surrounded by family. When I smiled and spoke to them, they were elated beyond belief. I was no longer crying. I was at peace. I praised the Lord for healing me. Suddenly, our senior pastor, Dr. Lester Spencer and teaching pastor, Janeese Spencer from our church, St. James United Methodist Church, appeared in the small area. I quickly remembered the words of James: "Is any one of you sick? He should call the elders of the church to pray over him and anoint him with oil in the name of the Lord. And the prayer offered in faith will make the sick person well" (James 5:14-15).

The pastors presented a beautiful blue prayer shawl with a white cross embroidered on it; the prayer shawls are part of the ministry of our church, offered in our times of need. A very special group of ladies sew and embroider God's blessings into the shawls. They have brought comfort and healing through Jesus in many instances. As the scripture states, I was anointed with holy oil as the prayer shawl covered my shoulders and they prayed over me, touching me and touching my heart. I immediately felt more alert and felt less pain. The pastors prayed for my ultimate healing, comforted me and thanked the Lord that I had survived. The anointing and prayers increased my healing. I continuously sang words in my mind and heart from one of my favorite praise songs: "I thank you for Your touch, I needed it so much."

I thanked them for their prayers and love and began to describe the "wake-up call" I had received from Jesus, praising Him for saving me and assuring me that my life would be different. Again, I apologized to the Lord for my selfish, self-centered, self-controlling prayer. I committed to obey His word and live according to His will, following His leadership in all I will do for the rest of my life. The pastors' visit helped me receive greater clarity. I realized that God is the source of our will; therefore we are able to work out God's will. I remembered this scripture, actually singing it in my mind:

> "Do you not know that your body is a temple of the Holy Spirit who is in you, whom you have received from God? You are not your own; you were bought at a price. Therefore honor God with your body" (1 Corinthians 6:19-20).

Many friends and other family members came by the hospital to check on me. By mid-afternoon, I was moved to a room in the cardiovascular unit and allowed to walk, eat and begin my new life in peace. I received precious and inspiring telephone calls all afternoon and all evening. Prayer warriors at our church confirmed their concerns and prayers for me. I could feel God's presence.

There was no fear in my heart even though there was still some minor pain. I actually rested and slept that evening, in spite of being awakened by nursing staff as they performed needed procedures. As I prayed, I asked Jesus to give me a clear message about my life, His desires and His plans for me. I prayed this prayer to our Father; "Keep me safe, O God, for in You I take refuge" (Psalm 16:1).

I realized how important listening to God is and how it would change my life and my approach to my problems and faith. I turned to this scripture and will always carry it in my heart:

> *"Now then, my sons, listen to me; blessed are those who keep my ways. Listen to my instruction and be wise; do not ignore it. Blessed is the man who listens to me, watching daily at my doors, waiting at my doorway. For whoever finds me finds life and receives favor from the Lord. But whoever fails to find me harms himself; all who hate me love death"* (Proverbs 8:32-36).

Healing continued to be God's work during my remaining days in the hospital. I felt very good, but sometimes when I got out of the bed at night to go the restroom, I would return to my bed with my heart thumping away in my chest. I mentioned it to nursing staff but medication did not seem to control the extreme heartbeat. Late one evening, as I lay in the hospital bed, hoping that my heart would calm down, I looked at the chair next to my bed and saw my beautiful blue prayer shawl, the white cross shining in the light. I grabbed it and held it to my chest. The thumping was corrected immediately and I quickly fell asleep. This condition occurred several times in the hospital and even after I had returned home. The prayer shawl was a miraculous healing instrument of our Lord. My heart was full of praise for His blessings on my life.

I was able to go home after only five days. Although my heart had not been damaged and I experienced a quick recovery, changes and adjustments in medications for my heart condition required longer monitoring and learning to follow new directions. Some weakness and problems related to new medication forced me to stay home for several more days after my release. But I did not worry at all. I committed the care of my body to Jesus to allow me to be available to do the work that He has planned for me. I was not anxious about returning to work, an unusual attitude for me.

I will always remember that God healed my spiritual body, not just my physical body. Changes in my life will be ongoing and I hope that my spiritual healing will affect the lives of others as well. We must consider that God's purifying love in our experiences of spiritual transformation include the deaths of our egos and the dark nights of our souls. In order for our lives to really be changed, we must let God's life grow in us and our old attitudes, fears, prejudices and self-centeredness must perish.

> *"I will not die, but live, and will proclaim what the Lord has done. The Lord has chastened me severely, but He has not given me over to death." (Psalm 118:17-18)*

CHAPTER 6

Focusing on Our Walk with Jesus

> "Be very careful, then, how you live—not as unwise, but as wise, making the most of every opportunity, because the days are evil." (Ephesians 5:15-16)

How did I ever develop my less than perfect relationship with the Father, the Son and the Holy Spirit? All my life I had called myself a Christian. I grew up in a small town in south Alabama, committing myself to the Lord at the time that many children recognize the Lord, participate in confirmation and join the church. I was active in our Methodist Church as a child and a teenager. I even graduated from a Methodist college in Montgomery, Alabama. In spite of the fact that I was a "long term" Christian, I did not have a personal relationship with Jesus. I could "talk the talk," but I really did not even know about "walking the walk."

Our wedding was a traditional Methodist ceremony in my hometown. After graduating and becoming a teacher, we purchased a house and were blessed with our children. As our family grew, we attended church on a regular basis, teaching Sunday school, organizing Vacation Bible Schools and performing other duties such as serving on committees. I "practiced" my Christianity on Sundays but reading my Bible was rare and my prayers were almost totally repetitious. Occasionally, I felt that I had experienced problems for the Lord to get my attention. Even at that time, I felt compelled to write down these messages and the minor changes that were results of the messages.

Every time we moved to a larger home to accommodate the growth of our family, a total of four children, we then moved to closer churches. We continued in the same mode as previously described: work and attendance. After our "nest" was almost emptied, we moved to a smaller home in east Montgomery. The distance to our church and some serious family problems that were causing us to doubt God's care became our excuses not to attend church. We all became very remote from God and from His church.

The story of our membership at St. James United Methodist Church is astounding. Several years after our move, our youngest daughter and I decided that we wanted to be "true Christians" and go to church on Easter Sunday (a good excuse for a new Easter dress, too). We planned to visit a Methodist Church in the eastern area rather than going so far into town to the church of our memberships. The church was fairly close to our home and had been recommended by friends.

At approximately eleven o'clock on Easter Sunday morning, we realized that we had not found the church we had planned to attend. Apparently, we had made a wrong turn and were not on the right road. To our surprise, St. James United Methodist Church was at hand and our time was running out. We decided that we would at least opt for this one-time visit because of the time and our commitment to attend church on Easter. When we entered the church, we were greeted and welcomed by a number of people. The service was more "contemporary" than I had ever experienced and I was fairly shocked by this modern Methodist Church, very different from the church to which we belonged at that time.

When the pastor began his sermon, I was very impressed by his passion and knowledge. This topic of the sermon was "forgiving your brother," a crucial and serious problem for me. Both of my parents had died within six months. My mother had Alzheimer's and had not been aware of what was going on for several years. My brother and his wife moved into my parents' home in the small south Alabama town to assist my father in caring for my mother and working with her care giver. Major remodeling and additional rooms were added to my family's home before they moved in with my parents. The deed for all property was signed over to my brother while the construction was underway to improve the timing and efficiency of the project.

From that point on, my father always asked me, "Now, has everything been corrected? Be sure you get that deed rewritten so that you get your share." I told my father not to worry about it. "My own brother wouldn't hurt me," I said. After their sad departures, I asked my brother if we could work out a fair plan. He said that we could talk about it. We finally agreed to a simple plan but it did not work out. After spending too much money on attorneys, I decided that my inheritance was not worth the effort.

At this time in my life, I thought about the property of our farmland that my parents had sold to send me to college. It was a gracious gift and I realized how good they had been to me; they had even chosen to name the street in the new area after me. I no longer wanted to experience conflict with my brother. However, we did not meet or talk for several years. If we happened to run into each other at a funeral or wedding, we spoke to each other politely and moved on to other groups. I continued to worry about our lack of a sibling relationship.

On that Easter Sunday, I was amazed at the sermon at St. James. Crying, I approached the pastor and said, "You were talking directly to me, sir." He responded with a smile, "No, m'am, I was not. God was speaking to you." I left the church in awe, thinking about God more than I ever had in the past. The scriptures included in the sermon stayed with me upon leaving the church: "Then Peter came to Jesus and asked, 'Lord, how many times shall I forgive my brother when he sins against me? Up to seven times?' Jesus answered 'I tell you, not seven times, but seventy-seven times'" (Matthew 18:21-22). A second scripture was even more inspiring, specifically addressing my spiritual needs:

> *"If anyone says, 'I love God,' yet hates his brother, he is a liar. For anyone who does not love his brother,*

> *whom he has seen, cannot love God, whom he has not seen." (I John 4:20)*

The Lord's words touched my heart and stayed in my heart, mind and soul from that moment forward. I remembered, "And when you stand praying, if you hold anything against anyone, forgive him, so that your father in heaven may forgive you your sins" (Mark 11:25). I acknowledged my own sins and began to pray for my own forgiveness, knowing that I would have to attend to these reminders. My husband and I began attending St. James regularly, moving our memberships within a few months, especially touched by an inspiring visit from our senior pastor and several visits from other members.

Shortly, thereafter, my uncle died and I planned to go to the funeral. I decided that I would contact my brother and tell him that I was going to forgive him. We met at my cousin's home after the funeral and I asked if we could talk later. He invited me to his home and I agreed to stop by "my old home" before I returned to Montgomery. I mentioned to my cousin that I was going to express my forgiveness. I was going to forgive him, my brother. Later, this verse, Luke 6:42 was a very important message for me, "How can you say to your brother, 'Brother, let me take the speck out of your eye,' when you yourself fail to see the plank in your own eye?" I began to realize that I am not perfect and that I had a plank in my own eye.

When I arrived, my brother had arranged a private time for us. I sat down and asked my brother to forgive me. The Lord had clearly told me to express my forgiveness in this way, asking for my brother's forgiveness, to secure the Lord's forgiveness for both of us. We continue to have a somewhat "distant" sibling relationship and maintain infrequent contact but at least we maintain contact. Birthday calls, Christmas cards and funerals describe our time together. When I think of my brother, I remember Colossians 3:13, "Bear with each other and forgive whatever grievances you may have against one another. Forgive as the Lord forgave you." Do you recall the ultimate forgiveness expressed by Jesus as He was nailed to the cross? He said, "Father, forgive them, for they do not know what they are doing" (Luke 23:34).

When I told my pastor what had happened, he gave me several tapes of other sermons on forgiveness. Read II Corinthians 2:5-11 to discern even more about forgiveness. Matthew 6:14-15, an enhancement of The Lord's Prayer, explains, "For if you forgive men when they sin against you, your heavenly Father will also forgive you. But if you do not forgive men their sins, your Father will not forgive your sins."

Our attendance at church continued but we did not have close contacts or relationships with other members and were not participating in activities other than worship services. We sat in the same seats every Sunday and began to really enjoy the praise music. We were soon approached by friends we had not seen in a long time and were invited to visit a Sunday school class. Our visit to the Shepherds of the Cross class was awesome. We immediately committed to join and have been faithful members since our first visit. The friendships that we maintain as a result of our membership have had a major impact on our lives. Our best friends are members of our Sunday school class; we fellowship together and assist each other in times of need. Our teacher, Bob Alred, has been an inspiration to us. The lessons that he teaches have increased our knowledge of the Lord and our relationship with Him. His own faith and love of Christ are prime examples for all of us.

Very soon after switching our memberships, our teaching pastor, Janeese Spencer, the senior pastor's wife, began a Women's Ministry, RENEW. I began to participate in this program from day one, still somewhat shy about the beautiful praise band music. I was rather shocked to see ladies my age raising their hands to the Lord as we sang, "Lord, I lift Your name on high. Lord, I love to sing Your praises." The RENEW ministry literally changed my life. I had considered myself an "involved" Christian but I was still not close to Jesus. The Rhema Bible Study and other aspects of RENEW definitely brought me close to Him, changing my thinking and many of my actions, giving up so many sins in my life.

I prayed for forgiveness of my sins, something I had never done seriously, realizing that Jesus really did wash our sins away. One of the most memorable and moving studies was learning about the

Old Testament and the building of the temple. We actually built a "temple" and toured and experienced the magnificent components of the temple. I shall always remember writing my sins on paper and burning them in the temple. That was probably the first time in my life that I really understood "forgiveness" and letting go of our sins.

RENEW has continued for eight years and I have missed very few Rhema meetings—only when I was hospitalized. I was drawn to the lessons and the fellowship of this program. I have learned so much from the lessons each year, more than I had ever experienced in my spiritual life up to this point. It is always obvious that the Lord has a direct message for the women and He speaks clearly through our pastor. You can always feel His presence in the sanctuary. I am willing to serve in any way to help this program continue to reach out to women all over the city. RENEW has touched the lives of hundreds of ladies, members of our church, members of other churches and some who had never met Jesus before this experience.

Worshiping God and being in His presence is a magnificent experience at St. James. Missing a Sunday service is very rare for my husband and me. The praise music is phenomenal; the members of the praise team are very talented. As I sing and listen to the songs each Sunday, I am moved by the way God is speaking to us. Most of us are clapping rhythmically during the songs; various people lift their hands to the Lord, move in rhythm and express extreme joy during the singing. I am frequently so moved by the words of the songs and the way that God is speaking to me that I cry throughout a song. Other members exhibit extreme joy and happiness while I cry. My tears are actually tears of happiness and appreciation. I am communicating with Jesus as these words touch my heart. One of the most impressive songs exemplifies what I experience in the worship, "God is awesome in this place." He is present and He is awesome.

At times, we find ourselves worshipping God with divided hearts and disinterested minds. We tune out the scriptures that we hear, the words of songs and hymns. We cannot really worship the Lord when our thoughts are focused on our problems, disappointments and desires. Because of the presence of the Holy Spirit at St. James, the love and passion of our pastors, members and visitors, it is very difficult not to experience true worship. I feel myself consecrating my heart to God as I enter the sanctuary at any time. I never leave a worship setting without God having rekindled my heart. On most Sundays, I approach the pastor with tears, expressing my appreciation and sharing what God's message meant to me.

"You are forgiving and good, O Lord, abounding in love to all who call to You. Hear my prayer, O Lord; listen to my cry for mercy" (Psalm 86:5-6).

CHAPTER 7

Focusing on Our Growth in the Lord

"Therefore, if anyone is in Christ, he is a new creation, the old one has gone, the new has come!" (II Corinthians 5:17)

Awesome and touching sermons each Sunday, powerful and inspiring lessons, contact with wonderful ladies in RENEW and small group support continues to change my life dramatically. I did not know what a real and personal relationship you could have with Jesus. I did not know how to pray, silently or aloud. I began to set aside a quiet time, reading my Bible almost daily and worshiping God from a different perspective. My focus on life and on God changed intensely. For the first time in my life I joined a small Bible study group. The lessons were intense and required dedicated daily reading and studying. An inspirational leader led the study, <u>Companions in Christ;</u> the small group, about twelve ladies and gentlemen, became very close. Surprisingly, I was able to handle all of the work that was required.

I began to journal and God began to speak to me through poems. As an English major, traditional poetry is one of my primary literary interests. Rhyming words and specific meter led me to write what the Lord was telling me. Sometimes I wrote poems based on scripture. Sometimes the poems addressed the stress and problems that I faced. Since that time, I have written hundreds of poems during my quiet time with Jesus. I know that God is speaking directly to me and encouraging me to speak to others in His name. Some of the poems were actually written to tell others about Jesus and all of the poetry has always increased my intimate relationship with Him. Occasionally, I reread poems that I do not remember having written, knowing that they are the word of God.

The Sunday evening small group meetings immediately assisted me in talking with the Lord, through prayer, poetry and scripture. I began to learn that I could sit quietly and listen to Him. I joined other small groups after Companions in Christ. The RENEW activities got me involved in several activities and my husband and I began to serve the Lord in our church as we continued to grow. I did not have the true picture, however, that there is no real intimate relationship without communication with Him throughout our lives. Do we remember that communicating is not just talking? Listening is an equally vital part of communication.

Several years ago, our church wide participation in <u>The Purpose Driven Life</u> increased small groups tremendously. The groups provided study of the purposes God has for each of us. An unexpected purpose arose when my cousin, Betty Cates (whom I had met for the first time at St. James), the education coordinator at St. James at that time, asked my husband and me to host a small group at our home for the Purpose Driven Life study. I could not refuse to host a group because we had recently moved from a fairly small garden home to a larger home to accommodate our growing family (six grandchildren by this time).

We had found a home in our own neighborhood and debated whether or not we should move. I prayed to the Lord to help us make the right decision. I committed the home to His service. I prayed that if He wanted us to move, He would work out the details. And He did—immediately. I further committed that I would use our new home to honor and serve Him. Our group is still meeting, after four years. The majority of the group has remained committed and we work very hard to study His word and offer prayers for each other and all of our church. We depend on each other, as we need prayer, face trials and have praise reports to celebrate. Our group is diverse, but our leader is excellent at leading us to the right studies and presenting inspiring lessons.

Another result of our church's participation in the <u>Purpose Driven Life</u> was the leading to a recommitment to the Lord. As a Methodist, I was baptized when I joined the church as a child At this time baptism was offered to all members who wanted to recommit their lives to Jesus. During a very moving RENEW meeting, (when I was miraculously participating in a praise dance, at my age), I recognized God's voice telling me that it was time for a recommitment. I signed up for the baptism. As a Methodist, I would never have dreamed that I could even consider an emersion baptism. This was definitely a step closer to the Lord. I very clearly remember stepping down into the cold water in the pool in the sanctuary in November. The water was cool, but as soon as I stepped into the pool and the pastors put their hands on me, I did not feel cold at all. As I was baptized, I felt intense warmth and a distinct renewal of my spirit. Becoming close to other members who were being baptized again was another blessing of this event.

RENEW has changed many lives in our city and has helped a lot of ladies overcome depression, addiction, not knowing Jesus, family problems, financial problems and resolved many other problems that separate us from Christ. Miraculous healing has occurred: marriages have been saved; babies have been birthed as answers to our pastor's prayers and the prayers of the great prayer warriors.

Esther's Women, another study in the women's ministry of St. James was inspirational for me, also, enhancing my relationship with Jesus. The Esther's group meets for a year, studying intensely, growing immensely and committing our lives to the Lord again, in all we do. The leaders of Esther's Women are extremely dedicated and provide exceptional leadership for the groups each year. We all grew spiritually and grew close together during the year of our study. We continue to care about each other and feel great appreciation to our leaders, Pam Miller and Leah Wynn.

The men at St. James experience the same moving growth in studies such as Joshua's Men, Numan and other opportunities. I have personally seen extraordinary growth in my own husband who has actually been a Methodist for only about 15 years. He even participated in the Emmaus Walk and has exhibited astounding growth in the Lord following that experience.

Working with the RENEW Leadership Team, greeting at various services, serving refreshments and other minor jobs helped me maintain my spiritual growth and know that I was serving God. Sometimes, I fussed at my husband for working too hard at the church. God spoke directly to me and said, "He's the kind of person who serves and helps others. This is how I keep him close to me." It never occurred to me that I also enjoyed being a servant of God. I got so much pleasure from my walk with the Lord and relationships with my Christian friends that I would never have considered letting go of one duty. I remembered what Jesus said, "…whoever wants to become great among you must be your servant, and whoever wants to be first must be slave of all" (Mark 10:43-44).

My most recent growth in my walk with Jesus was the opportunity to become a Stephen Minister. When St. James began solicitation for applicants, I picked up a registration form and took it home with me. I prayed and prayed about my decision to apply. Finding time to complete the fifty hours of training, follow-up studies and performing the needed duties for care receivers was the only thing interfering with an immediate commitment. Then I remembered how much a Stephen Minister had helped my daughter in another city. I was not sure, however, if I could complete the training and duties of a Stephen Minister while maintaining my job and other duties. This scripture led me to my decision, "For whoever wants to save his life will lose it, but whoever loses his life for me and for the gospel will save it" (Mark 8:35).

Sometimes our idea of being a servant is different from Jesus Christ's idea. His idea is that we serve Him by being the servant of others. I was very concerned about making the right decision in order to serve Him and to serve others. I turned to Psalm 4:5, "Offer right sacrifices and trust in the Lord." Through that scripture, God spoke very clearly to me as I completed the form. I knew that this was a mission that God had chosen for me. Stephen Ministry was a big message for me. I increased my intimacy with Jesus while studying, listening to our inspiring leaders and looking at my own life as I learned how to help others.

Reading and discussing books with topics such as caring for others, becoming assertive Christians and helping care receivers come close to God greatly enhanced my knowledge and my own relationship with Jesus. Very specific knowledge was provided to increase my walk with the Lord. I was reminded again that Jesus wants us to serve Him by being the servant of others. I remembered that the testing of the saints was not preaching the gospel but washing disciples' feet. I hope that I will be able to come close to the description of Stephen in Acts 6:5, "They chose Stephen, a man full of faith and of the Holy Spirit."

> *"If Your law had not been my delight, I would have perished in my affliction. I will never forget Your precepts, for by them You have preserved my life." (Psalm 119:92-93)*

CHAPTER 8

Focusing on Our Problems

An anxious heart weighs a man down, but a kind word cheers him up. (Proverbs 12:25)

Our church has kept my husband and me in touch with the Lord over the years, even during frustrating times. Many prayer warriors and our pastors provided the stability to help us maintain our relationships with Jesus, not giving up when things went wrong. Our family members joined us in worship several times, even joining the church! I was particularly concerned about the teenagers when they were living with us, feeling that they would come close to Jesus through participation in activities with their peers, even though they were members that they did not yet know. I prayed daily for Jesus to take over and remove this problem that I could not fix.

However, I continued to worry, approaching them, sometimes "preaching" to them, and sometimes arguing with my husband about decisions that needed to be made. I cried all of the time. My co-workers often commented that I seemed to be very distressed. I feared for my family, especially the grandchildren who faced a challenging time in their lives. I still did not attend to the scripture about seeking "first His kingdom and His righteousness, and all these things will be given to you as well" (Matthew 6:33). I really paid no attention to the next verse, "Therefore do not worry about tomorrow, for tomorrow will worry about itself. Each day has enough trouble of its own" (Matthew 6:34).

We see these worries and know that we certainly have enough troubles, but do we ever look at it from this perspective? We continue to worry about tomorrow, don't we? Later I was led to this scripture in James 4:13-15:

> *"Now listen, you who say, 'Today or tomorrow we will go to this or that city, spend a year there, carry on business and make money!. Why, you do not even know what will happen tomorrow. What is your life? You are a mist that appears for a little while and then vanishes. Instead, you ought to say, If it is the Lord's will, we will live and do this or that.'"*

I really feared for the lives and the spirits of my family, saying that I was turning the problems over to Him, usually praying and then saying, "It is in God's hand." But did I really believe that God was ultimately in control?

Worrying about today and tomorrow, I continued to talk to the Lord almost every moment of every day. I prayed about decisions, asking for signals to let me know what to do. Not waiting patiently for His assistance, I always tried to resolve the problems myself. In reality, I removed myself from His Holy hand. During this very stressful time, I definitely could not "find" time for my quiet time in the mornings. I became extremely exasperated because of so many problems that were not being resolved but were growing at home and at work. Now, I always refer to Matthew 8:26-27 when Jesus calmed the storm:

> *"He replied, 'You of little faith, why are you so afraid?' Then He got up and rebuked the winds and the waves, and it was completely calm. The men were amazed and asked, 'What kind of man is this? Even the winds and the waves obey Him!'"*

When God answered my prayer, I knew that my problems had overtaken my life on earth and my life with Jesus. In the emergency room and in the ICU, I did not worry. I knew that God was caring for me. His miraculous love was spread over me. I felt Jesus' love and presence in the hospital. I will always remember I John 4: 18-19:

> *"There is no fear in love. But perfect love drives out fear, because fear has to do with punishment. The one who fears is not made perfect in love. We love because He first loved us."*

At the beginning of my heart attack, I had recognized that I had to trust Him and depend on His love in all aspects of my life. I will remember Romans 8:9 forever, "You, however, are controlled not by the sinful nature but by the Spirit, if the Spirit of God lives in you." At that moment, I willingly turned my life over to Jesus. I would have been happy about whatever happened because I knew that I now acknowledged His will and He loved me.

I truly turned my problems over to Him. We try to control our lives but God invites us to open our hearts to the eternal flow of His spirit. My problems were not really troublesome as I recall this scripture:

> *"Because he loves me,' says the Lord, I will rescue him; 1 will protect him, for he acknowledges my name. He will call upon me, and I will answer him. I will be with him in trouble, I will deliver him and honor him. With long life will I satisfy him and show him my salvation'" (Psalm 91:14-16).*

We cannot simply recall the scripture; it has to be imbedded in our hearts. Our heart is the place of our deepest knowing.

"Look upon my suffering and deliver me, for I have not forgotten Your law." (Psalm 119:153)

CHAPTER 9

Focusing on Our Recovery

"Remember the wonders He has done, His miracles, and the judgments He pronounced." (Psalm 105:5)

God's healing is miraculous! I began to feel better and better. As I recovered every day, I searched my Bible for His direct messages to me. I turned to the fourth chapter of Jonah, remembering about his life and trials. Jonah 4:3 shook me when I read it again. Jonah had prayed, "Now, O Lord, take away my life, for it is better for me to die than to live." Again, in verse eight, a plea for dying was approached: "He wanted to die, and said, 'It would be better for me to die than to live." We don't know how Jonah responds when the story ends but we can proceed to find what is in our hearts. And the same request had been in my heart! During this time of fear and tribulation, I should have repeated, "So we say with confidence, "The Lord is my helper, I will not be afraid" (Hebrews 13:6). But I was afraid, especially for my family. I did not depend on God's grace but gave up and followed Jonah's decision.

But at the time of my "wake-up call," I began to trust in God's willingness to care for me. I knew that I was in His hands and my will shall always be only His will. As I went through recovery, even the minor pain and inconvenience of treatments did not disrupt my immediate intimacy with the Lord. The prayer warriors, pastors, counselors, friends and mentors from my church began to visit me on the first day of my hospitalization, coming to the ICU and to my assigned room. I was literally overwhelmed by their thoughtfulness and loving care. We know that our family members and friends love us but we usually don't have time to listen to them or appreciate their loving concerns for us.

After monumental intercessory prayers, I began to realize that a renewed relationship with God should become the chief change in my life. I knew that I must increase my capacity for Him. I thought about the name, "Abba"; Jesus was the first one to call God Abba (Father). I recognized that life is not a problem to be solved. It is a journey and God wants us to be intimate with Him on our journey. I prayed my prayers of thanksgiving for His love as I lay in that uncomfortable hospital bed.

My cardiologist reconfirmed the diagnosis that there had been no damage to my heart, that I would be released from the hospital very soon and must continue to take my medications and commit to frequently scheduled pro time tests (something that I had never done consistently). The doctor again stated that there was really no explanation for the heart attack except that a blood clot had obviously caused the problem but had been broken up before damage had been done. I thought about the story of Jesus healing the demon possessed man and what He had said to him,

> *"As Jesus was getting into the boat, the man who had been demon possessed begged to go with Him. Jesus did not let him, but said, 'Go home to your family and tell them how much the Lord has done for you, and how he has had mercy on you.' So the man went away and began to tell in the Decapolis how much Jesus had done for him. And all the people were amazed." (Mark 5:18-20)*

My family and friends were in awe because of my recovery and healing. Sometimes they expressed concern that maybe I had not been healed and was not well. But I knew that I was. God does not lie to us. I remember that "Because He himself suffered when He was tempted, He is able to help those who are being tempted" (Hebrews

2: 18). And I had definitely been tempted—tempted to follow my ways, not His will. Friends and co-workers came by, crying over my problems, but leaving with smiles at my healing. I knew that I would survive to complete His plan for me because of this message: "Peace I leave with you; My peace I give you. I do not give to you as the world gives. Do not let your hearts be troubled and do not be afraid" (John 14:27). I sincerely recognized that we find peace in the loving arms of our father. I was reawakened by this scripture, "Submit yourselves, then, to God. Resist the devil, and he will flee from you" (James 4:7).

The message I received at this time was that I must share this blessing with many others. I heard a calling to try to inspire as many people as possible with this story. As I lay in the hospital bed, frequently alone and peaceful because of the New Year holiday, the words, "Heart of the Matter" came to my mind. I again recalled the scripture to which I am so frequently led, "When I called, You answered me; You made me bold and stouthearted" (Psalm 138:3). My calling was confirmed when I was led to this Psalm, "My heart is stirred by a noble theme as I recite my verses for the king; my tongue is the pen of the skillful writer" (Psalm 45:1).

I hope that I am a skillful writer and that this book is speaking to you! I am reciting my words as Jesus is leading me to do. Read and listen to His word.

> *"Though I walk in the midst of trouble, You preserve my life..." (Psalm 138:7)*

CHAPTER 10

Focusing on God's Will in Our Lives

"We must pay more careful attention, therefore, to what we have heard so that we do not drift away." (Hebrews 2:1)

Everyone who visited me or telephoned me at the hospital expressed concern about my "work addict" life, fearing that my working habits, family stress and even my devotion to God was the cause of my heart attack. More than one person prayed with me and encouraged me to consider giving up my job, changing my life in a positive way and even abandoning some of my services to the Lord and to my church. I was reminded that the body is not separate from the soul; "lectures" abounded, reminding me that I must take care of my body if I am to continue growing spiritually. Proverbs 4:26-27 reminds us that we must "Make level paths for your feet and take only ways that are firm. Do not swerve to the right or the left; keep your foot from evil." What causes us to swerve away from Him? Is it our worries, our compulsions, our anxieties?

When we become overwhelmed by problems such as overworking, we generally focus only on what we consider most important. The challenges we face can cause the separation from our Lord and Savior. Our problems and pleasures often overshadow our ability to let His word take root in our inner being. I was definitely one who wandered away from my journey with God by becoming distracted by anger, envy or by my personal failures or successes. Unaccustomed to listening, I let God's messages to me go unnoticed. These frequent failures that we experience are times when the Lord sends challenges to obtain and retain our attention.

These challenges can result in something good for us. As I listened to my dear friends in Christ, I began to wonder if God had a reason for me to leave my job and spend more time at home and in my religious work. The prayers and recommendations that were made to me led me to the Lord again for the first time in a long time. I began immediately to pray for His will to be clear so that I could follow His plan for me, follow Him in all I do, every day of my life. I began to realize that when my life was at the edge, I turned to the Lord in prayer and He heard me! As I prayed, I recalled Psalms 33:20, "We wait in hope for the Lord; He is our help and our shield. In Him our hearts rejoice, for we trust in His holy name." I turned to Him to discern His will for my life, my heart rejoicing as I began once again to "trust in His holy name."

I felt confident as I began searching my Bible for His direct word. My confidence was reinforced by His word as He led me to the perfect scriptures as He always does to provide me with His perfect answers. Hard choices have to be made in our lives at times. But to make good choices, we must "...fix our eyes on Jesus" (Hebrews 12:2). I was led to this scripture to help me return to trusting Him:

> *"This is what the Lord says: 'Look I am preparing a disaster for you and devising a plan against you. So turn from your evil ways, each one of you and reform your ways and your actions.'"*
>
> *(Jeremiah 18:11).*

The message was clear to me. I recognized that I had to change my life. I must know His word and follow His word in every aspect of my life, turning away from evil, reforming my spiritual and earthly life. I loved my job but I was willing to consider giving it up at this time if that was God's plan for me. To reform my actions, I had to listen to His word and let Him help me resolve all problems and discomforts in my life.

I began searching more deeply for His messages. God always leads me to open my Bible to His word—His word about the needs in my life, when I take time to listen to Him. I automatically opened my Bible to the book of Hebrews. As I prayed for His voice to speak to me, I remembered a proverb: "Commit to the Lord whatever you do, and your plans will succeed" (Proverb 16:3). Our responses to God during and after crises can be unexpected and they can lure us to Jesus. How have we gone through some of these disasters?

As I read the book of Hebrews, I clearly recognized God's voice, talking to me directly. This verse stayed in my mind and in my heart even as I read the other verses: "You need to persevere so that when you have done the will of God, you will receive what He has promised" (Hebrews 10:36). Persevering is a word that really touched my heart. God allowed me to continue my life and He wants me to persevere in all ways, according to His will. Another confirmation was in Hebrews 6:12, "We do not want you to become lazy, but to imitate those who through faith and patience inherit what has been promised."

A compulsive, obsessive control freak is rarely ever "lazy," but I was willing to turn my life over to Him and retire and "cool" according to His will. I felt a calling to continue to work and serve others but I continued to pursue His word to discern His message, each and every word. I was encouraged by the idea that God does not expect me to go at it alone. He does not expect me to find my own way and strength to continue working while implementing real and lasting changes in my life. He gave me the Holy Spirit. He will guide, lead and empower me to live the Christian life that He wills. But I have to be willing to yield control to Him and let Him lead me. I was thrilled by this message in Hebrews 6: 9, "Even though we speak like this, dear friends, we are confident of better things in your case—things that accompany salvation." Isn't that an amazing and empowering thought that our lives will be better with our salvation? We take it for granted, don't we? It is definitely a thought that should always be imbedded in our spirits but sometimes it is not and then it becomes amazing and empowering!

I will always remember that it is not my will, but His will, to which I must attune my heart. Philippians 2:13 confirms this thought, "...for it is God who works in you to will and act according to His good purpose." I had to ask, "God, what do you see when you look at me?" During those peaceful hours in the hospital, I sat quietly in His presence to wait for the Lord to respond. Sometimes our impatience pushes us to take control away from God, but it did not happen this time! We do not know how or when God will respond but my patience overcame my impatience and I did not try to take control away from Him. I did not get nervous waiting for the Lord's answers to my questions.

As I read these verses, I began to realize that God was specifically telling me to keep working for Him and with Him, persevering until He brings another plan to me. It was reaffirmed that sometimes God uses negative circumstances to achieve His divine purposes. I know that with God's involvement, what seems like defeat can become a "door to live." His messages for me to continue serving Him and serving others were even more clearly telling me that I must change my life if I am to do His will, His way. I envisioned major changes in my "life style," as much as in my life.

Reading and memorizing the verses from Hebrews, I moved on to other books in the New Testament. Even with ongoing visits and telephone calls from sweet friends and co-workers, I found that I had more than enough time to research His will and commit to Him. I remained alert and awake for most of the day and a lot of time at night. I found more confirming words about perseverance in the book of James:

> *"Perseverance must finish its work so that you may be mature and complete, not lacking anything." (1:4)*
>
> *Blessed is the man who perseveres under trial, because when he has stood the test, he will receive the crown of life that God has promised to those who love Him." (1:12)*

Perseverance is part of faith. I knew that my faith was not being challenged. My faith was being confirmed. I know that the Lord sends me passages that I need to read and speaks His word to me through my reading of His word and listening to his Holy voice. More messages about the collaboration of faith and work are sent to us through the book of James, "What good is it, my brothers, if a man claims to have faith but has no deeds? Can such faith save him?" (2:14); "In the same way, faith by itself, if it is not accompanied by action, is dead." (2:17); "You see that a person is justified by what he does and not by faith alone." (2:24); "Anyone, then, who knows the good he ought to do and doesn't do it, sins" (4:17).

Just as the word of the Lord came to Jonah, the word of the Lord came to me. In Ecclesiastes 3:22, He gives us a terrific message, "So I saw that there is nothing better for a man than to enjoy his work, because that is his lot. For who can bring him to see what will happen after him?" God wants us to enjoy our lives, our jobs, our discipleship, and our families. Things are not always perfect, even when we are walking with the Lord. We must remember that God has limits and expectations.

And He expects us to have limits and expectations in our lives. "The Teacher" clearly explained this concept in Ecclesiastes 3:1, "There is a time for everything, and a season for every activity under heaven." We must look at our life styles and let our Father show us what is constructive, beneficial and when the season is here for certain activities. It was very clear to me that I must change many parts of my life to better serve Him and others. I felt peaceful about His messages as I read His word. I knew that I would have to let the Holy Spirit work in my life. I cannot do it alone—and I am going to quit trying. We have to experience these "wake-up calls" in our lives to see and hear the plans that our Father has for us. It is better to get these clear messages under very trying circumstances than to never receive His message. At times we have to quit "doing," don't we, and stand still and pay attention to His message?

I continued to pray, to seek His will. I was not making decisions until I found explicit answers in scriptures to which he led me. After reading and praying over the concerns that had been expressed to me,

I became even more peaceful and focused on Him. His message was that this is not a perfect world and things will not be perfect on this earth but God still has a plan for each of us. I was encouraged by this verse from Ecclesiastes 1:15, "What is twisted cannot be straightened; what is lacking cannot be counted." But we frequently continue to try to straighten out things, don't we?

Ecclesiastes 7:13-14 says, "Consider what God has done: Who can straighten what He has made crooked? When times are good, be happy; but when times are bad, consider: God has made the one as well as the other. Therefore a man cannot discover anything about his future." We must trust in Him. I felt peaceful about all of His word that I was reading and taking into my spirit. I knew that I would have to let the Holy Spirit work in my life. Again, I realized that I cannot do it alone—and I have quit trying.

> *"Though I constantly take my life in my own hands, I will not forget Your law" (Psalm 119:109).*

CHAPTER 11

Focusing on Our Gifts

"Each one should use whatever gift he has received to serve others, faithfully administering God's grace in its various forms." (I Peter 4:10)

God's perfect gift at this time of my life was the explanation of His plans for me to follow His holy will. I did not make any decisions until I found explicit answers in scriptures to which He led me. After reading and praying over the concerns of my heart and the concerns expressed to me, I became peaceful and focused on Him. He reaffirmed the knowledge that there is a plan for each of us on this earth, a plan that we can complete if we follow His will.

Again, we are reminded by scripture in Ecclesiastes 1:9 that we will suffer in this imperfect world but all of these things happen again and again, "What has been will be again, what has been done will be done again; there is nothing new under the sun." We must simply trust in God at all times, in all situations. Life is not perfect, but with faith we receive mercy and grace, the ultimate gifts from our Father.

We must trust Him to use the gifts He has provided to us. Think about this scripture, "Do not call anything impure that God has made clean" (Acts 10:15). The blood of Jesus washes us clean—what a gift! I will be happy as I turn over my pleasures and my problems to Him so that He can lead me in the right direction. I know that I can trust our Redeemer. I know that God loves us so much that "He gave His one and only Son, that whoever believes in Him shall not perish but have eternal life" (John 3:16). Sometimes we take this familiar scripture too casually. What greater gift could ever be given for us and to us?

I thought more and more about the gift of life that our Father has given us. The gift of eternal life is even more astounding. Then I thought about the second chance of life on earth that had been presented to me. How peaceful I felt! I knew that I would let the Holy Spirit work in my life according to His will.

I acknowledged His word to me. His message to change my life is definitely a gift. The opportunity to serve Him and serve others with Him is an unimaginable gift. I know that a life with Christ is a life of faith, as confirmed by this scripture, "And without faith, it is impossible to please God, because anyone who comes to Him must believe that He exists and that He rewards those who earnestly seek Him" (Hebrews 11:6). Faith is both belief and trust, depending on God. Living out faith can be hard especially in the uncertainties of our world. We must remember that "Faith is being sure of what we hope for and certain of what we do not see" (Hebrews 11:1). Grace and peace are also gifts from our gracious Lord. When we are afraid or discouraged, we must remember these very familiar verses about grace and peace:

> *"Grace and peace to you from God our Father and the Lord Jesus Christ." (Galatians 1:3)*

> *"Grace and peace be yours in abundance through the knowledge of God and of Jesus our Lord. "(II Peter 1:2)*

> *"Grace and peace to you from God our father and from the Lord Jesus Christ." (Romans 1:7)*

A common statement about God is that He works in mysterious ways. We frequently see all good things as a "mysterious" act of God. How can we forget that there are no mysteries about God's work on this earth and in our lives? He definitely has plans for us and a purpose for life on this earth. We also often refer to the fact that God can use bad things to do good things. But do we always recognize how He does this or even believe that He does it? My stay in the hospital was a wonderful example of bad turning into good. My life with Jesus was changed as described in former chapters. My life with others on this earth was greatly improved. It would be difficult to report how many people prayed for me, visited me, and sent me flowers, food and other precious gifts.

One of the most awesome gifts from God was the contact with so many people, reaffirming that they cared for me and loved me. I was literally overwhelmed by some of the telephone calls and visits. Numerous cousins with whom I had not talked in years called me and expressed their love and concern for me; I was elated. My brother and his wife drove to Montgomery to visit me in the hospital. Their visit touched my heart because of our distant relationship, even after our forgiveness events. My caring aunt and uncle drove up from my hometown, confirming their love and concern for me. Friends, other family members and co-workers continued to show their love and care by calling, visiting and sending such encouraging gifts. Plants that I water and admire today remind me of the wonderful, supportive friends and family.

We have many friends in our lives, but many times we do not take time to communicate with them on a regular basis. I had certainly neglected numerous friends and not bothered to make contact with neighbors and acquaintances for a number of years. The visits, telephone calls and sweet cards from so many people touched my heart and made me realize that God expects us to be friendly, to care about our friends and family in a positive, active way.

Invoking a blessing means calling upon the "God of Truth" to pour out His grace for a particular purpose. Invoking a blessing is an act of faith; it is confidently claiming a promise inherent in God. We invoke blessings, but more importantly, God lays blessings on us. At this time, I referred to this scripture, "Make vows to the Lord your God and fulfill them; let all the neighboring lands bring gifts to the One to be feared," (Psalm 76:11).

"He has scattered abroad the gifts to the poor, his righteousness endures forever." (Psalm 112:9)

CHAPTER 12

Focusing on Commitment

"If you remain in me and my words remain in you, ask whatever you wish, and it will be given you." (John 15:7)

As I studied His word and focused on Him during my hospital stay, I received a clear message that I needed to streamline my lifestyle to have more time for solitude, prayer and reflection. I thought about the fact that Jesus lived in the world, but not of the world. I was being called to streamline my life in numerous ways. There are times when old things must be abandoned because a new beginning is necessary.

Before I was released from the hospital, I had to make a commitment to Jesus to live according to His will. I spoke with my senior pastor and teaching pastor again, receiving encouragement about making the right decisions. Our associate pastor, Walter Albritton, came to visit and pray with me at the end of my stay, warming my heart. He placed my prayer shawl over my shoulders and reached out to place his hands on me as we prayed. A very strange "electric" shock hit me when he touched me. I really felt the presence of God in that hospital room. I thought about how I might see God's hand in my new life. He will definitely touch me and I will feel His touch. Walter has always touched my heart with his faith and love for our congregation. I felt God's touch through him.

I thought about this scripture we read in Romans 15:13, "May the God of hope fill you with all joy and peace as you trust in Him, so that you may overflow with hope by the power of the Holy Spirit." I asked myself, "How does my life reflect my trust in God so that I may experience His righteousness?" I knew that I must make a significant commitment to change my life in order to live in His will. Making vows to Him came to my mind and my lips. I quickly remembered the very familiar scripture from Ecclesiastes 5:5, "It is better not to make a vow than to make a vow and not fulfill it." I thought that I had always understood this particular scripture, but it was made even clearer under my current circumstances. I said to myself and to Jesus, "Whatever I commit, I am going to do it to the end. I will persevere according to Your will and Your love and mercy."

The events of our lives are like pieces of a puzzle, separate and apart. But when they are put together, they make us the persons that we are. We would probably be astounded upon seeing that puzzle put together. Current events of my life had certainly come together like pieces of a puzzle, forming a person I did not recognize or want to be.

I remembered another verse, "Therefore do not be foolish, but understand what the Lord's will is" (Ephesians 5:17). I know that the Lord said the heavens are higher than our ways, and His thoughts are higher than our thoughts. I was ready for the commitment to change my life.

My vow to Jesus will never be abandoned. I am committing all portions of my life to Him: work, testimony, service, family, friends, and writing. Most importantly, I will never turn away from His word. I will be open to His calling in all aspects of my life. I will listen to Him as I meditate and communicate with Him. I remember this verse from a Psalm of David: "My guilt has overwhelmed me like a burden too heavy to bear," (Psalm 38:4). But I know that my burdens will never be too heavy to bear. The blood of Jesus washes us clean and God takes our burdens upon His yoke. "Praise be to the Lord, to God our Savior, who daily bears our burdens." What a blessing!

I will continue to pray for the families of my four children, that they may hear God's message, too, and always commit their lives to Jesus. I am praying for each of them by name, giving Him my concerns and expressing my love for each one of them, children and grandchildren. I am not getting stressed out, however, when I cannot control their lives. I am convinced by my "wake-up" call that the Lord will take care of my family in His time, the best time for changes to occur. I really mean "I am putting it in Your hand" this time.

> *"I have taken an oath and confirmed it, that I will follow Your righteous laws," (Psalm 119:106)*

PART B

The Heart of the Matter

Focusing on God's Will....
Focusing on Changing Our Life Styles

> *"Who is wise and understanding among you? Let him show it by his good life, by deeds done in the humility that comes from wisdom. (James 3:13)*

I could have thanked the Lord for His grace and mercy and continued in my current lifestyle. My excuse would have been, "Well, He chose to save me. I don't have to change anything. He loves me just like I am." It is true, God loves us. But He wants us to live a life with Him, in Him and for Him. He definitely has purposes for all of us if we will listen to Him. The changes in my life will be based on this scripture from Colossians 3: 1, "Since, then, you have been raised with Christ, set your hearts on things above, where Christ is seated at the right hand of God. Set your minds on things above, not on earthly things." My focus had to change! I had been focused on earthly things and concerned about my control of things for a long time. Isn't it easy to do this all of the time, unless we focus on Him?

Part B describes the changes that have already occurred in my life and might also occur in your lives, the changes that are in progress and the changes that will come according to His will and in His time. These changes may not yet be evident or even imaginable. In all aspects of my life, I am going to follow His word in Hebrews 3:12, "See to it, brothers, that none of you has a sinful, unbelieving heart that turns away from the living God." What can draw us away from God? We must always depend on Jesus. We must get to the heart of the matter every day! If we do not focus on His will, we fall short of being who God wants us to be and doing what God wants us to do.

> *"I have sought Your face with all my heart; be gracious to me according to Your promise. I have considered my ways and have turned my steps to Your statutes." (Psalm 119:58-59)*

CHAPTER 13

Increasing Our Intimate Relationship with Jesus

"And everyone who calls on the name of the Lord will be saved." (Acts 2:21)

My "wake-up call," the revelations from Jesus and my eventual commitments to follow the Lord's will, definitely resulted in major changes in my life style. Many of the changes are external and observable while many of the improvements in my life are spiritual and may not be noted by others. But I know that they have already been witnessed and acknowledged by Jesus Christ. Changes in our lives also can create changes in the lives of others. Positive changes develop when we trust in our Father and submit to His will, giving our lives to Him. Through our suffering and the tests that we experience, we can draw nearer to God.

As I read my Bible, prayed and listened to God while I was in the hospital, I realized that having an intimate relationship with Him means communicating with Him. Communicating is reading His word and praying; perhaps more importantly, a real and intimate communication is listening to His voice, following His lead in all aspects of our lives. Now I hear His voice very clearly. I was guilty of avoiding the time I had dedicated to communicate with the Lord. Overcome by so many problems and distresses, I did not take time to meet with Him and read His word on a consistent basis. For several months prior to the experience of my "wakeup call," I had practically abandoned my quiet time and meditation. I continued to pray throughout the day and at bedtime, but my prayers were prayers of desperation, only sometimes offering Him praise for His goodness.

Now I have committed my "quiet time" to Jesus. I promised that I would maintain my improved relationship with Him. In the hospital and after returning home, I have not missed one day of talking with our Lord. Even more astounding is the fact that I have arisen before 5:30 on work days in order to start my day with Him. I have not missed time with Him one day, even on Saturdays when I am prone to sleeping later than usual.

Saturday mornings are very special as I read His word, pray, meditate and listen to very moving praise music. My Saturdays have changed tremendously because of starting the day in this manner. Saturdays have always been happy days, days of some rest but nothing like the Saturdays of my life now. I start the day in a happy mood, praising God as I look at the miracles of His word and His world, ending my day in a happy and joyful mood. Following His lead to now go to bed at a decent hour on Friday nights has helped me to arise at a reasonable time on Saturday mornings to enjoy His presence, starting my day like any other day, dedicated to Him.

My prayer time has changed in other ways, too, after reading <u>Reordering Your Day</u>, written by Dr. Chuck D. Pierce, a book recommended through our RENEW studies. Our teacher, Janeese Spencer, was teaching us about the prayer watches detailed in the Old Testament. Because of the lessons and reading the book, I have discovered that God calls to me at unexpected times, maybe midnight or often at 3:00 AM, to offer my prayers and listen to His loving voice. I have found that this is not a tiring time but an inspiring time; reordering my day reordered my spiritual life. My awakening early each morning and starting my day praising Him has greatly increased my relationship with Jesus.

The Lord consistently leads me to the scriptures that I need in order to understand His plan for me and to follow His will. I am virtually amazed at the messages that are so clearly spoken to me. As I watch the sunrise each morning, I happily repeat this verse,

"This is the day the Lord has made; let us rejoice and be glad in it" (Psalm 118:24). Honestly, every day after my "wake-up call I have been happy, even when I am faced with trials and difficulties. I trust in the Lord, I have faith in His grace and mercy. I will never again abandon my commitment to Him. I will persevere and remember what James said; "The Lord is full of compassion and mercy" (James 5:11). Now I am developing a habit of looking for and following the Holy Spirit's lead.

My recommitment to the Lord has changed my attitude in many instances and aspects of my life. I know that I am not perfect. I know that I may have a close relationship with Jesus, but I will still make mistakes, still sin. I have to force myself to give up my compulsive behavior and extreme judgment of others. Since my release from the hospital, I have been singing a song in the shower that came to me right after returning to my home. As I shower, I sing to myself, "Wash me clean, Lord, wash me clean. Take all of my sins away. Wash me clean, Lord, wash me clean. It will be a brand new day." The tune is consistent. I move in rhythm as I sing this song, truly believing that God is washing my sins away—truly believing, also, that I have sins every day that need to be washed away. I pray constantly that God will "Wash away all my iniquity and cleanse me from my sin" (Psalm 51:2).

Let us remember that "God's peace in our hearts brings cleansing and refreshment to our minds and bodies," as stated by Billy Graham. To ask for forgiveness, we must acknowledge our sins. Turn to Psalm 32:5 and read, "Then I acknowledged my sin to you and did not cover up my iniquity. I said, 'I will confess my transgressions to the Lord'—and You forgave the guilt of my sin."

This is an important concept for us to consider every day as we live our lives, even when we are focusing on Jesus, for "Who can say, 'I have kept my heart pure; I am clean and without sin'"? (Proverbs 20:9) We are still human beings and who can ask that question and not think of even a small problem that would keep us from being called clean and pure at heart? Sometimes we make the right decisions; at other times we think that we have made the right decision but we are far away from what God wants from us.

Let's think about Proverbs 21:2, "All a man's ways seem right to him, but the Lord weighs the heart." If I knew that the Lord was going to "weigh" my heart at certain times, I know that I would need to get new scales or start a major diet. I would not even want to see the results. How do you feel about God "weighing" your heart?

Drawing closer to God means letting go of the things that have held me away from Him; things like compulsiveness, workaholic behavior, frustration and trying to control family, friends and co-workers. When I make decisions about anything, I must ask for His guidance, waiting patiently for His response. One of the most critical scriptures to which we must always adhere is found in Romans 12:2, "Do not conform any longer to the pattern of this world, but be transformed by the renewing of your mind. Then you will be able to test and approve what God's will is—His good, pleasing and perfect will."

We must also remember to worship and praise Him for His pleasing and perfect will! Let us follow His will and remember that sometimes we can turn God's blessings into a show of vanity, frequently ignoring our source of all goodness. Read II Kings 20:1-14 about how Hezekiah was blessed during his illness and how he reacted to the Lord's grace, turning God's grace into a show of vanity. When we receive spiritual or physical recovery, or both, as I did, we can learn more about our relationship with God and grow in our relationship through our responses, outlooks and behaviors. As Paul said, "Since we live by the Spirit, let us keep in step with the Spirit. Let us not become conceited, provoking and envying each other" (Galatians 5:25-26).

"The Lord is close to the broken hearted and saves those who are crushed in spirit." (Psalm 34:18)

CHAPTER 14

Focusing on Our Work in the World

> *"God is not unjust; He will not forget your work and the love you have shown Him as you have helped His people and continue to help them. We want each of you to show the same diligence to the very end, in order to make your hope sure." (Hebrews 6:10-11)*

Other changes that have occurred in my life were the result of my consultations with my Christian friends, prayer warriors, co-workers and family—but most importantly, my message from the Lord. When I received God's confirmation that He has a purpose for me in this world, it was very clear that in order to maintain my job and continue to participate in so many activities, I would have to maintain my life in a very different way. I will always reflect on this verse in I Timothy 1:12, "I thank Christ Jesus our Lord, who has given me strength, that He considered me faithful, appointing me to His service." We must always remember that He appoints us to His service and that we must listen to Him and follow "His will."

My returning to work was a concern of all family, friends and even co-workers. Everybody was afraid that the stress of my job had caused my heart attack and might cause another one. I, however, was confident that I am now in the Lord's hands and that His love will always be with me. I cannot forget His word in this portion of

Hebrews 13:6, ..." What can man do to me?" Whether I am at work or in another environment, I know that God is there, too, because He said, "Never will I leave you; never will I forsake you" (Hebrews 13:5). He keeps His promises! I had to remember, too, that returning to work did not have to be a rerun of what had occurred in the past three months. Remembering this scripture was a bonus for me, "Forgetting what is behind and straining toward what is ahead, I press on toward the goal to win the prize for which God has called me heavenward in Christ Jesus" (Philippians 3:13-14).

I had to deal with major problems and concerns at my school after the first of the New Year—a new year for me in many ways. I did not despair. I did not become discouraged or depressed even when people lied and plotted to cause problems. When I face uncertainties, I no longer become anxious; I present my requests for sensible answers and support, in His time and in His way. I always thank our Father at the time of my request.

Another major problem in my job was the need to always maintain control just as I did in all other aspects of my life. I have finally been able to delegate tasks and duties appropriately and trust in those on whom I depend. I finally acknowledge that I am not a genius. I know that I am not the only person who can complete the requirements of my position. I simply have to trust in others as I trust in the Lord. I am no longer going to be a compulsive control freak. We must trust in our Lord who is described in I Corinthians 14:33, "For God is not a God of disorder but of peace." We cannot find peace if we are rushing, fussing, pushing every day in our lives, at work or at home.

I am no longer taking major projects home with me—I am doing what I can at work and letting other staff do their jobs. This is really a miracle for me and unbelievable to many people! I am now using time at home to be with my husband, spending more time with my precious grandchildren, communicating with the Lord, writing what I know that Jesus is telling me to write and even watching some of my favorite old television shows. Using my time in a more reasonable manner means that I do not have to stay up until the wee hours of the morning to get chores done. I know that my projects will be completed because Peter tells us in I Peter 5:7, "Cast all your anxiety on Him, because He cares for you." God knows what we are facing and He cares for us! We must be confident!

God wants us to fulfill His will, but He wants us to be well and happy, too. I was led to this scripture, "Let us not become weary in doing good, for at the proper time we will reap a harvest if we do not give up" (Galatians 6:9). Work, therefore, cannot overtake all aspects of our lives. We must live in Him and He in us, always finding time for all of our commitments to Him, not just doing our money making jobs.

Another important change in my work habits involves my working hours. In the past, I worked very late every afternoon, convinced that I must get jobs completed before the next day. Adhering to my follow-up doctor appointments and regularly scheduled blood tests has assisted me in reorganizing my time schedule for each day. I have stayed late very little since my "wake-up call" and return to work. The only afternoon that I stayed very late, I was hurrying home in a heavy rain. When traffic stopped at my exit on the interstate, I severely rear-ended the truck in front of me. I was absolutely devastated, thinking about getting soaking wet in the middle of all the traffic on the interstate while awaiting the arrival of the police and all of the other problems related to an accident.

As I got out of the car, I held my cell phone in my hand and told the gentleman whose truck I had hit that I would call the police. He looked at me and said, "Wait a minute. Let's look at it first." We looked at his truck and my SUV and saw no damage! After slamming into his truck as hard as I had, no damage was a miracle! He also said, "Don't worry, its fine." I thanked the Lord with my first breath and hugged the man's neck, saying, "God bless you!" Another "wake-up call": "Don't wait until after dark to go home, daughter. Remember your commitment to improve your life." I took that message very seriously and I have been going home at reasonable times since that evening.

I felt His message that He still has a plan for me to complete projects at school and work hard to improve the lives of the students who count on all of us to make their lives better. I recently read this statement made by Viktor Frankl, "...a person with a *why* to live can sometimes survive almost any how." I think that my experience confirms this statement. Don't we ask the Lord "why" many times when things happen in our lives?

Another confirmation absolutely astounded me very soon after my return to work. I had developed a serious case of strep after my stay in the hospital and once again had to stay home for a couple of days. My associate called me to remind me of a special event, a beautiful fashion show exhibited by our wonderful students in their wheelchairs, planned for that Wednesday morning. She encouraged me to come if I could because the teachers and students wanted me to attend the presentation. I arrived at work expecting just a time to be asked to step forward and make a few remarks.

But that is not what happened! Before the fashion show, I was called forward and presented with a certificate as the nominee and winner for the CEC Alpha Brown award for Special Educator for the state of Alabama. I was speechless, something that surprised everyone! The board member, Dr. Laura Carpenter, who had nominated me for this award and my associate Cynthia McCaghran, who had helped gather the letters of recommendation really touched my heart. The school also presented me with a gift certificate for the stay in the hotel in Birmingham and food for the weekend of the presentation. They had already told my husband about the award and he had secretly planned to spend Friday and Saturday with me during this honorable time.

I have never been so honored. I certainly would not have expected to receive such a prestigious award at my age and at this time in my career. Again, the Lord confirmed my purpose for working with children with disabilities. I will persevere to the end! God wants us to persevere, following His will. We must remember to "Never be lacking in zeal, but keep your spiritual fervor, serving the Lord. Be joyful in hope, patient in affliction, faithful in prayer. Share with God's people who are in need" (Romans 12:11-13).

I have committed to continue to do my job until the Lord tells me it is time to quit and move in another direction. I already envision His plan for me: to continue working for another year and then commit myself to continuing His discipleship in the way that He leads me. God expects us to always work in some way, never to simply relax and ignore His purposes. In II Thessalonians 3:10-12, God reminds us that He wants us to work with Him and through Him, "For even when we were with you, we gave you this rule: if a man does not work, he shall not eat. We hear that some among you are idle. They are not busy; they are busybodies. Such people we command and urge in the Lord Jesus Christ to settle down and earn the bread they eat."

As we commit to follow His will, we can be assured that the Lord will be with us and His help will always be at hand. Remember that when we are following His commandments, He is always supporting us as confirmed in Deuteronomy 30:11, "Now what I am commanding you today is not too difficult for you or beyond your reach." How refreshing to read that scripture! God does not give us tasks that are too difficult if we listen to His word and follow His guidance. But we often only think of our own plans, don't we? Let's refer to this scripture when we are concerned about our daily plans and the "big picture" of our lives, "Many are the plans in a man's heart, but it is the Lord's purpose that prevails" (Proverbs 19:21).

Our plans must be His plans. We will then live our lives for Him, improve our lives and the lives of many others, reaching out to them or setting an example for them. As Paul tells us in Colossians 3:17, "And whatever you do, whether in word or deed, do it all in the name of the Lord Jesus, giving thanks to God the Father through Him." Paul is definitely an example of doing work in the name of the Lord Jesus, isn't he?

> *"Blessed are they who keep His statutes and seek His word with all their heart." (Psalm 119:2)*

CHAPTER 15

Focusing on Our Health

"But I will restore you to health and heal your wounds." (Jeremiah 30: 17)

I listened very carefully to His challenge and calls for me to do His will. "Slowing down" and taking care of my physical and spiritual lives were also very clear messages from the Lord. Getting up earlier in the mornings and spending quality time with my Father encouraged me to go to bed at a more reasonable time. In the past, my bedtime was rarely before midnight, frequently stretching out to two or three o'clock in the mornings. I have found that going to bed between nine and eleven o'clock has made a significant improvement in my life, at night and during the day.

Let us remember these words in Psalm 4:8, "I will lie down and sleep in peace, for you alone, O Lord, make me dwell in safety." We can all have more peaceful sleep and avoid the stressful nights when we are unable to sleep if we turn to Him for our peace. Is this not a true statement? "Rest—the things that will be done will be done in God's time." Let's rest in God and contemplate the beauty and mystery of life. During this time of struggling to reorder my life and get an appropriate amount of sleep, I have learned to go to sleep peacefully, leaving all of my problems for a new day. I recently was referred to these words in Psalm 3:5, "I lie down and sleep; I wake again because the Lord sustains me." He sustains us all.

I have given up my compulsive behavior and no longer force myself to complete all of my tasks at night as I always did, even when I had actually been too tired to complete those multi-tasks. We all know that we have responsibilities that require our attention and our efforts, but we cannot let those responsibilities take over our lives. I can certainly testify to that! We should remember that Jesus knows what we are doing and why we are worrying at all times. This is confirmed in Psalm 139:1-3, "O Lord, You have searched me and you know me. You know when I sit and when I rise; You perceive my thoughts from afar. You discern my going out and my lying down; You are familiar with all my ways." We must rest in God to be able to live our lives according to His will. This verse is easy to remember because it is so relevant to this concept, "Find rest, O my soul, in God alone; my hope comes from Him" (Psalm 62:5).

Eating more healthy food was a great need in my life. I have given up on so much of my unhealthy eating and need to overeat. I will always remember that my "body is a temple" and I am going to honor the temple. My anxiety to eat, eat, eat when I am distressed has greatly decreased. I have focused on healthier foods such as fruits, vegetables and less fattening meats, limiting my intake of sugar and carbohydrates. We must remember that we have to be dedicated to Him in order to commit to a healthier life. If we don't follow His word, we cannot maintain the healthier life that we need. Proverbs 19:27 confirms this perspective, "Stop listening to instruction, my son, and you will stray from the words of knowledge." We are very tempted by good foods and good times; we must be committed to eat healthier and honor our bodies and our Father.

Following the requirements and recommendations of my doctors has been equally important and produced positive results in my physical life. I no longer neglect to keep appointments, especially the necessary blood tests (even if they are weekly). The Lord took care of me in times of trouble and I will not forsake His will. I know that He expects us to take care of ourselves and honor Him in all we do, not just at times of praise and worship. I will give thanks to Him for difficulties I have faced because He used these physical problems and my other difficulties to strengthen and purify my body, both physical and spiritual. Tragedies, illnesses and many other kinds of problems are used to give us gifts of strength, endurance, patience, increased faith and deeper wisdom. And I needed deeper wisdom and increased faith at this time of my life.

Although I am usually a very busy person, always multi-tasking, never just relaxing, I realized that I do not get the exercise that my body needs. I never "had" time and never took time." This is another commitment that I have made in changing my life style. To keep my spiritual heart healthy, I must keep my physical heart healthy, also. In Romans 7:14-15, we learn, "We know that the law is spiritual; but I am unspiritual, sold as a slave to sin. I do not understand what I do. For what I want to do, I do not do, but what I hate I do." If we want to be physically healthy, we must love the exercise and healthy habits of life, doing what we "want to do," being healthy, rather that doing what we do to make us unhealthy (hopefully what we hate).

I will commit to follow His will in regards to my health because God is such a good and gracious God. I did not experience any damage to my heart. I knew that God's hand had healed me on my way to the hospital. I still envision Jesus putting His hand on my body and the blood clot breaking up without any surgery at all. During my stay in the hospital, my cardiologist, a dedicated and very knowledgeable doctor, said that she did not know exactly what had happened. She could only report that there was evidence of some "debris" of the clot. When I returned for my follow-up visit, she again explained that she could not really diagnose what had happened but she again assured me that there was no damage to my heart! Psalm 18:16 describes what happened, "He reached down from on high and took hold of me; He drew me out of deep waters."

After my return from the hospital, I developed some symptoms of strep throat: fever, headache, sore throat and a serious rash. I followed His leadership again and went to the doctor, was diagnosed with strep and followed the recommended procedures for curing the strep. Once again, I had to stay home a few days in order to overcome this illness. I did not force myself to go to work. Several weeks later, I developed another sore throat with severe pain in my neck and ear. Again, I returned to the doctor and was shocked to be diagnosed with Bell's Palsy. I had never heard of the symptoms, but the material that I was given to read clearly confirmed an accurate diagnosis.

Again, I had to miss a few days of work. But when the doctor approved my return and I felt well enough to cope with the stress of my job, I returned to work. I shocked many people when they saw the paralysis on the left side of my face. I could only drink with a straw on the other side of my mouth, my left eye would not close and I suffered a lot of pain, having to bandage that eye several times.

I could have been very embarrassed about the paralysis that lasted for almost a month. Putting on lipstick was hard, eating and drinking were hard and smiling was hard. But at this time, I smiled more than I ever have in my life! I felt very blessed by this illness. It was another confirmation for me that Jesus cares for us. We read in Psalm 54:4, "Surely God is my help; the Lord is the one who sustains me." This illness may look bad, but the good part of it is that it goes away! The prescribed medication worked and I was back to normal in three or four weeks. People have expressed a lot of surprise at how the symptoms of the Palsy went away. I know that, "In my anguish I cried to the Lord, and He answered by setting me free" (Psalm 118:5).

Bell's Palsy sometimes leaves us with various ongoing problems; for example, I still have a small hearing problem which is being addressed by my ENT, but I am still thankful to our Lord that this is my major problem at this time. When I get a little frustrated trying to hear certain tones, I think of this scripture, "Therefore we do not lose heart. Though outwardly we are wasting away, yet inwardly we are being renewed day by day" (II Corinthians 4:16). I actually feel His renewal of His spirit in my heart and body every day.

> *"Therefore my heart is glad and my tongue rejoices; my body also will rest secure." (Psalm 16:9)*

CHAPTER 16

Focusing on Our Families

> "If anyone does not provide for his relatives, and especially for his immediate family, he has denied the faith and is worse than an unbeliever."
> (I Timothy 5:8)

Caring about my family and caring for my family has always been a major portion of my life. My serious concern about my children and grandchildren was something I focused on almost every hour of each day. I did not trust in the Lord and obviously did not truly believe that Jesus would take care of the situation if I turned it over to Him, even though this was a always a focus of my prayer. I was not giving Him trust in every aspect of these concerns. At last, I finally obeyed His word and surrendered my fears to Him. Today, I continue to pray in faith and knowledge that He will take care of the needs of my family, relieving me of my great stress and frustration.

When thinking of my reluctance to trust the Lord enough to turn these family problems over to Him, I remember the story of Job. His story is really a drama that addresses the reality of Job's suffering more from the crisis of lack of faith that was going on within him, than from the struggle of what was happening to him externally. But Job persisted in loving God. We find ourselves tempted to doubt

God's goodness, mercy and love and we pray for help without real faith.

Unexpectedly, our daughter and grandchildren decided to return to their homes and restart their lives. This decision was not mine to make. I did not have any control over the move and did not try to control any of the decisions. I must admit that I miss them very much and continue to pray for their joy and peace every day. I look forward to the day that the Lord has chosen to show His love and support to them. I am no longer the control freak who tries to manage all aspects of my life and the lives of others.

God has blessed my husband and me with four wonderful children and eight very special grandchildren. We recently learned that we will become great grandparents this year. I will continue to pray for each of them every day, never giving up on the Lord's presence and mercy. In Romans 5:5, Paul reminds us that "...hope does not disappoint us, because God has poured out His love into our hearts by the Holy Spirit, whom He has given us."

Families are definitely the "heart of the matter" in all of our lives. Jesus does not want us to abandon our families but to love them through Him. Our families are affected by the way we treat them, how we make decisions and most importantly, how we live our own lives. Paul gives us an example in I Corinthians 10:31 32, "So whether you eat or drink or whatever you do, do it all for the glory of God. Do not cause anyone to stumble..." Sometimes our care can actually cause family members to stumble. We are examples for each other. We must always pray to make a difference in the lives of our family members.

Think about how we may have helped make them who they are. Do we see positive results or negative concerns because of our influences on their lives? Have we nurtured our family members spiritually? Have we actually been spiritual guides? We know that God ultimately works through troubled families to accomplish His will, but many times our conflicts and lack of love for each other separate us from Jesus, as it has at times in my family. We are never perfect because we are only human beings making choices, hopefully choices led by our Father. We will try to follow this message from

Matthew 5:48, "Be perfect, therefore, as your heavenly Father is perfect." When I think about my family and how they were raised spiritually, I wish that I had had a closer relationship with Jesus and understood His will, impacting their lives in a more positive way.

Love for our family members must be a primary focus in all of our lives. John tells us a very important message about love in I John 4:7-12:

> *"Dear friends, let us love one another for love comes from God. Everyone who loves has been born of God and knows God. Whoever does not love does not know God, because God is love. This is how God showed His love among us: He sent His one and only Son into the world that we might live through Him. This is love: not that we loved God, but that He loved us and sent His Son as an atoning sacrifice for our sins. Dear friends, since God so loved us, we also ought to love one another."*

Is this scripture not amazing? Can we imagine offering such magnificent sacrifices for members of our family? Would we consider giving our lives or the lives of our children to save others? Sometimes we have to offer sacrifices, but not such awesome sacrifices, in order to save the life of someone in our family.

Family disagreements and differences can cause conflicts in our lives and our family relationships. We must always follow Jesus' leadership and not enable our family members to live as He does not want them to live. I Timothy 3:4-5 gives us vital information about family care, "He must manage his own family well and see that his children obey him with proper respect. (If anyone does not know how to manage his own family, how can he take care of God's church?)" Caring for our families means making Jesus the focus of our lives. Remember, as we deal with these situations, that Jesus said, "Take care of my sheep," John 21:16. To care for our families and His "sheep," we must seek the will of God in all we do.

My commitment as a result of my "wake-up call" is to commit my life to Him and commit my family to Him. I cannot be manipulated if it is not His will. I will offer all problems to Him. I will offer my family needs to Him for His guidance and support in all areas of our lives. Let us read I Corinthians 13 to be reminded of God's powerful love for all of us and how we should express our love for our families. God loves our families and knows our needs.

My commitment to my family is to spend more time with all of them—those nearby and those far away. I am very disappointed in myself when I think of some relatives with whom I have had no contact in months or even years. Family is an important part of all of our lives. I am committed to spending more time with my grandchildren; I am making more frequent contact with those who are not around all of the time. I am going to maintain this commitment because I know that it is a request of our Lord.

A major commitment in caring for my family is not in action but in prayer. I continue to pray for our children and grandchildren in a specific and faith-believing way each day. My prayers begin with asking God's blessing on them and ends with confirming their needs. The major difference in my prayers, however, is in putting it in God's hands, leaving Him in charge of the answers and timing of the answers for my family. When we release our needs into God's hands, we free ourselves to do what God is asking us to do.

> *"God sets the lonely in families." (Psalm 68:6)*

CHAPTER 17

Focusing on Our Friends and Neighbors

"After David had finished talking with Saul, Jonathan became one in spirit with David, and he loved him as himself. From that day Saul kept David with him and did not let him return to his father's house." (I Samuel 18:1-2)

Our friends are also vital components of our lives. I have found it very difficult sometimes to find the time to devote to important friendships. My family, my job, my compulsiveness and my own interests have frequently prevented my spending any quality time with important people in my life. At times, I have thought about a list of my friends and found it distressing that the only friends I could mention having had contact with recently were the people with whom I work. Those friends are very important to me but I had to search my mind and heart deeper to identify the other friends of my life.

Friends are a treasure to us, aren't they? They give us happiness and hope and help us enjoy our lives in ways that we cannot enjoy things alone. Remember this statement from Jesus, "Love each other as I have loved you. Greater love has no one than this, that he lay down his life for his friends" (John 15:12). We are commanded to love our friends. Jesus loves us. Let's love them.

Another verse comes to my mind when I think of my lack of participation in activities with the friends of my life, "Dear children, let us not love with words or tongue but with actions and in truth." (I John 3:18) Yes, words are better than no contact at all; telephone calls, cards and letters keep us in touch with our friends from whom we are separated. As this scripture states, however, we must show real love in these "actions" and include face to face meetings. His truth must shine through us as we maintain our contacts with our friends. Our light is important to our friends just as our friends are important to us, "You, O Lord, keep my lamp burning; my God turns my darkness into light" (Psalm 18:28).

We find great happiness in the friendships of those we trust. We find great joy in having someone with whom we can speak on terms of equality, never fearing condemnation or lack of trust, knowing that we can share the secrets of our hearts. When we think about the relationship between David and Jonathan, we might think of someone with whom we have a relationship that binds us together. Remember this scripture in Proverbs 17:17, "A friend loves at all times." Never forsake your friend, the friend of our Father. Mutual love, respect and admiration are characteristics of this kind of friendship. Let's think of the many gifts that are the result of our trusting friendships and use our human friendships to help us cultivate a deeper friendship with Jesus Christ. God is our greatest friend. How can we enhance this friendship?

Paul, in I Thessalonians, details his affection for the Christians in Thessalonica. He is open about his affection for them, wanting to be their guide and religious instructor. He is proud to be their friend; his affection is very endearing. Imagine receiving a letter from a friend, someone that you wished you could sit down and talk with because he or she is a great listener and can help guide you in the right direction. Many cards that I received in the hospital contained messages about spiritual life and my relationship with Jesus. These special cards expressed my friends' loving concern for my physical and spiritual life. These uplifting cards helped increase my prayer time with the Lord.

When our lives are filled with pain and challenges, we have greater need for the support of our friends in Christ. We may respond to these hardships by taking refuge in materialism, abandoning God, becoming addicted to a variety of things or being very hard and bitter. Jesus offers us another way to deal with our problems as we are comforted by friends as described in Hebrews 10: 24-25, "And let us consider how we may spur one another on toward love and good deeds. Let us not give up meeting together, as some are in the habit of doing, but let us encourage one another—and all the more as you see the Day approaching." This is definitely what my friends did for me!

I have maintained more contact with friends and have had innumerable opportunities to share my "wake-up call" with them. I am committing to be even more reliable about being a friend. I will refer to this scripture to maintain this promise: "When a man makes a vow to the Lord or takes an oath to obligate himself by a pledge, he must not break his word but must do everything he said" (Numbers 30:2). I have started with telephone calls and am following up with personal visits, lunch times and other opportunities to enjoy our fellowship. This verse from Proverbs 18:24 reminds us of the value of friendship, "A man of many companions may come to ruin, but there is a friend who sticks closer than a brother."

Neighbors should be our friends, too. I must confess that I do not really know my neighbors, even those who live right next door and unfortunately, this is not uncommon in our busy world. In my active life, I have not taken time to get to know my neighbors and cannot even remember their names. Proverbs 3:28 reminds us of how kind and helpful we should be to all of our neighbors, "Do not say to your neighbor, 'Come back later. I'll give it to you tomorrow.'" One of the most touching things that happened during my illness was a sweet and inspiring card I received from a next door neighbor with whom I usually had no contact. After my return from the hospital, I had an opportunity to speak to my neighbor in the yard and express my thanks. I am going to maintain this friendship by reaching out to my neighbor as she and her family did to me.

After I began my exercise by walking several times a week, I hoped that I might have contact with other neighbors during my "outings." On a Saturday morning, I chose to walk earlier than usual because a storm was anticipated in the afternoon. I walked out the back door and started down toward the golf course. Seeing a group approaching the nearby hole, I chose to go around the house and walk on the sidewalk, in fear of being hit by a golf ball. I immediately ran into a neighbor walking her dog. We spoke and began a conversation. During our talk, my neighbor, who recognized me, revealed that her husband was from my hometown. We had a great conversation and I intend to follow up on this relationship. We think God works in mysterious ways but actually He has a plan, from which He works, to benefit us and improve all of our lives. Proverbs 3:29 describes the relationship we should maintain, "Do not plot harm against your neighbor, who lives trustfully near you."

As a result of these changes in my lifestyle, I have made a serious commitment to be "neighborly" to my friends and neighbors. The love we show to others is the same love that we experience from knowing Jesus Christ. God's love enables us to live with and to love one another. Paul tells us in Romans 15:1-2, "We who are strong ought to bear with the failings of the weak and not to please ourselves. Each of us should please his neighbor for his good, to build him up." God makes us strong as we increase our relationships with Him.

Another change that his been fascinating is my speaking to everyone with whom I come in contact. It is amazing how conversations can be started and enhanced with strangers. We may simply be talking about the weather, a bargain at a sale or any common topic. Many times, however, the conversation will evolve into talking about Jesus. I have shared my "wake-up" call on numerous occasions, seemingly obtaining the attention and interest of those who are listening to this brief story. Simply smiling at people that you meet or face makes a big difference, also.

We need each other, don't we? Our Christian community supports us when we have needs and we support others in turn. If we allow God to lead us, we will find many opportunities to be evangelists.

> *"I will remember the deeds of the Lord; yes, I will remember Your miracles of long ago." (Psalm 77:11)*

CHAPTER 18

Focusing on His Service

> *"Then Jesus came to them and said, "All authority in heaven and on earth has been given to me. Therefore go and make disciples of all nations, baptizing them in the name of the Father and of the Son and of the Holy Spirit, and teaching them to obey everything I have commanded you." (Matthew 28:18-20)*

God has a purpose for each of our lives. He wants us to serve Him and reach out to others, bringing them to Him. Evangelism is a scary word for some people. But it is definitely the plan He has for us. We are the lamp to those with whom we come in contact. Luke mentions this concept several times: "No one lights a lamp and hides it in a jar or puts it under a bed. Instead, he puts it on a stand, so that those who come in can see the light" (8:16). Again, the lamp of our body is mentioned in verse 11:33, "No one lights a lamp and puts it in a place where it will be hidden, or under a bowl." Jesus does not want us to "hide" our lamps or not persevere in our service for Him.

At the time of my "wake-up call," I had to ask myself this vital question: "Who is God inviting me to be? What is He inviting me to do?" As my previous testimony reveals, I knew that I was not close to God at the time of my "wakeup call"; I had thought that I was and even testified to many people about my relationship with Jesus. But

I did not have the intimate relationship with Him that would answer these questions. I had to remember again that life is not a problem to be solved, but a journey. God wants us to be intimate with Him in our journey, following His will. Intimacy means communicating with God at a deeper level than my life was allowing me to do. We must work on communication every day.

We know that prayer is communication with God and part of prayer is listening. We must come to know His voice. Remember that Jesus was the first called to God to have an intimate relationship with His Father.

How eager are we to hear Him as He talks to us? How can we listen to Him? In order to increase our intimacy, we must learn to listen. Sometimes pride keeps us from admitting that God is not in control of our lives. We don't want to admit that we need Him or that He should be the primary focus of our lives. Ephesians 2:8-10 explains how we can overcome these problems:

> *"For it is by grace you have been saved, through faith—and this is not from yourselves, it is the gift of God—not by works, so that no one can boast. For we are God's workmanship, created in Christ Jesus to do good works, which God prepared in advance for us to do."*

Christianity is doing great things with God, not for Him. Our lives must reflect the process of our work with Him more than any finished product of which we may boast. We must be a living sacrifice, dedicating our daily actions and habits of mind. Righteous actions and attitudes are evidence of our commitment to Him. Sometimes this is difficult for us, isn't it? Remember Hebrews 2:18, "Because He himself suffered when He was tempted, He is able to help those who are being tempted." When things are not going right in our lives, we must depend on Him. Jesus said to Martha, when she was angry that Mary was focused on Jesus and not on helping her:

> *"Martha, Martha,' the Lord answered, you are worried and upset about many things, but only one*

> *thing is needed. Mary has chosen what is better, and it will not be taken away from her.""* (Luke 10:41)

I remember, again, that God does not expect us to go at it alone. In the past, when I faced problems, I usually said this quote, "If God will bring me to it, He will bring me through it." I certainly believe this statement more than I did prior to the "wake up call". He does not expect us to find our own way and muster up enough inner strength to implement the real and lasting changes in our lives. He does not expect us to be His disciples without Him. He gave us the Holy Spirit. He guides us and empowers us to live the Christian life that He designed for us. But we have to be willing to yield control to God and let Him lead us. In my "wake up call," I received the message that in order to improve my relationship with God I would have to let Him become the chief part of my life. I would have to begin by increasing my relationship with Him.

Are we willing to hear all that God has to say to us, even when we may consider it unpleasant? How is God speaking to us? How do we know if we need to participate in any opportunity that is presented? The answer to these questions is in Micah 6:8, "He has showed you, O man, what is good. And what does the Lord require of you? To act justly and to love mercy and to walk humbly with your God." Do you remember when Jesus said to Matthew, "Follow me," when Matthew was sitting at the tax collector's booth? "And Matthew got up and followed Him" (Matthew 9:9). Paul points out in Romans 10:17 that faith comes from hearing the word of God, "Consequently, faith comes from hearing the message, and the message is heard through the word of Christ." A life with Christ is a life of faith!

"If anyone wants to be first, he must be the very last, and the servant of all," (Mark 9:35). Jesus made this statement to the disciples after they had been arguing about who was the greatest among them on the road to Capernaum. Yes, God does expect us to be His servants. Don't forget that at times our pleasures and problems can overshadow our abilities to let His word take root in our inner beings. This "shroud" allows God's word to be hidden from us, definitely an effect of our sins. We are also unaccustomed to listening and we let

His message go unnoticed. Remember the explanation of the parable of the seed in Luke 8:11-15. He wants the seeds that He has planted in us to grow as the seeds that fell on "good soil," for the "seed on good soil stands for those with a noble and good heart, who hear the word, retain it and by persevering produce a crop" (Luke 8:15).

How do we sense God's affirmation about being called to be a servant? We must listen to His messages! Sometimes we are afraid to listen, aren't we? We fear what God may say to us. We must remember that we are all still beginners and always will be—until we join our Father in heaven. But remember, also, that we are called to be different, to be set apart, to become His followers. Jesus loves us and God has a plan for our lives. We must listen and follow Him. King George said, "The secret of happiness is not to do what you like to do, but to learn to like what you have to do." In Philippians 2:12, Paul explains that we cannot work out our own salvation with the Lord: "Therefore, my dear friends, as you have always obeyed—not only in my presence, but now much more in my absence continue to work out your salvation with fear and trembling, for it is God who works in you to will and to act according to His good purpose."

> "Those who know Your name will trust in You, for You, Lord, have never forsaken those who seek You." (Psalm 9:10)

CHAPTER 19

Focusing on Our Personal Commitments

"However, I consider my life worth nothing to me, if only I may finish the race and complete the task the Lord Jesus has given me—the task of testifying to the gospel of God's grace." (Acts 20:24)

As I considered making a commitment for His service, this scripture came to my mind, "For God is greater than our hearts, and He knows everything" (I John 3:20). Yes, I thought, He knows everything about me. He knows my mind, my heart, my faith, my sins and everything else about me. Sometimes that is scary, but when we recognize that He can use all diversity in our lives in a positive way, it is all right for Him to know us. We need His knowledgeable will in our lives. Working for Him and with Him is a blessing and a privilege for us.

In the first verse of the third chapter of Ecclesiastes, we read the familiar words about "a time for everything and a season for every activity under heaven." Verses 9-11 describe how God uses work, "What does the worker gain from his toil? I have seen the burden God has laid on men. He has made everything beautiful in its time. He has also set eternity in the hearts of men; yet they cannot fathom what God has done from beginning to end." We probably cannot fathom what wonderful plans He has for us.

Titus says in Chapter 3, verse 14, "Our people must learn to devote themselves to doing what is good, in order that they may provide for daily necessities and not live unproductive lives." What is an unproductive life? In order to follow Jesus and begin a truly productive life, sometimes we must abandon old things; a new beginning is a necessary thing. Do we need to worry about what was left behind when we start over?

> *"Let us fix our eyes on Jesus, the author and perfecter of our faith, who for the joy set before Him endured the cross, scorning its shame, and sat down at the right hand of the throne of God,"* (Hebrews 12:2).

Did Jesus worry about His past? Remember what He said as stated in Luke 23:46, "Jesus called out in a loud voice, 'Father, into Your hands I commit my spirit.' When He said this, He breathed His last." Can we even come close to a new beginning like this?

At the time of my "wake-up call," I realized that it is important to look at where I have been, but it is even more important to look at where God is taking me in my spiritual life. In Psalm 143:5, David said to the Lord, "I remember the days of long ago;" I meditate on all Your works and consider what your hands have done." I realize that I must streamline my lifestyle so that I have more time for solitude, prayer and reflection, living in the world as Jesus did, rather than "of the world" as we frequently do.

We must look at the "word within the word." Let's think about this question: "Will a simple, modest lifestyle prepare us to live as Jesus did?"

Since my release from the hospital, I have not missed one day of rising to be with Him. I have streamlined some aspects of my life and continue to work on others. I know that my message was serious. I remember these words of Jesus in Matthew 7:26, "But everyone who hears these words of mine and does not put them into practice is like a foolish man who built his house on sand." I ask myself, "How can I stand firm?" Ask yourself this question: "What can we do to be sure that our house is not built on sand but on the rock of our savior?" Instead of merely desiring changes in our lives, we must all be transformed into His likeness.

My house will be built on sand and will certainly be washed away if I do not follow His will. Our personal commitments must be His personal commitments for us. I read the scriptures to which I am led every morning and at other times. I hear the message. I stop and listen. I continue to pray for the positive changes in my life to continue, that I will trust Him, put my problems in His hands and stop worrying and fretting. In order to commit myself to Him, I have given up at least two jobs at my church and it has been a blessing to allow other people to step in and serve Him. I will continue to serve Him as He directs me. The changes in my work lifestyle allow me to follow His will and spend more time with Him.

Sometimes I still get frustrated, even as I continue to increase my intimacy with God on a daily basis. I continue to pray and to seek His blessings. Let us remember that sometimes we have opinions about things and God sees them in other ways. We want things but we don't get them. Why? James tells us in James 4:3, "When you ask, you do not receive, because you ask with the wrong motives, that you may spend what you get on your pleasures." That verse should be a "wake-up call" to all of us. Our motives are not always positive; our understanding is not always clear. That is why we must trust in His will and follow Him in all we do, honor Him in all we do and this will make a difference in our lives. It will remind us of this scripture, "For where your treasure is, there your heart will be also" (Matthew 6:21).

I know that I must abandon my own desires, forget the things I would like to boast about, forget my disappointments and anxieties, and recall this scripture: "Those who live according to the sinful nature have their minds set on what that nature desires; but those who live in accordance with the spirit have their minds set on what the Spirit desires" (Romans 8:5). My intimacy with the Lord is helping me to recognize what the Spirit desires. I want to commit only to His will and let go of my own sinful desires.

Jesus referred to the prophet Isaiah when He said, "These people honor me with their lips, but their hearts are far from me" (Mark 7:6). God wants our love to be authentic; He wants us to be persons whose hearts match our words, our actions and our beliefs. He does not want us to be hypocrites.

I want my commitment to be so sincere that I always listen to Him speaking to me. God speaks to us and God shows us what to do. He transforms His written word into living word—just for us! The fruit of the spirit is "love, joy, peace, patience, kindness, goodness, faithfulness, gentleness and self-control. Against such things there is no law. Those who belong to Christ Jesus have crucified the sinful nature with its passions and desires" (Galatians 5:22-24). Let us ask God how to live in the Spirit and experience these amazing fruits. Catherine of Siena said, "The actions of the Savior are so rich in meaning that every soul that ponders them finds in them its own share of spiritual food."

I continue, at times, to be compulsive, judgmental, envious, expecting all things and all people to be perfect. I pray constantly for God to capture my tongue and my mind, to remove these ungodly characteristics. I see His support more and more each day. I have found that I can be friendly and nice to acquaintances and strangers and quit thinking about how I look or how they look. I want to be like Jesus one day. I have to remind myself of this scripture every day, a Psalm of David, "Who can discern his errors? Forgive my hidden faults" (Psalm 19:12). And we all have hidden faults, don't we? We don't recognize all of our sins; we don't acknowledge all of our sins. The only solution to our problems is the Holy Spirit, living in us.

How do you see God's hand in your new beginning? Here are some suggestions that will help all of us. Following these guidelines, we will be able to continue to increase our relationship with Jesus and live our lives according to His Godly will:

1. Look at where you have been and where God is taking you.
2. Pray prayers of questions: what are God's desires for you, instead of always praying answers to Him.
3. Pray for courage and strength to face your problems rather than always praying to be released from your trials.
4. Cultivate a heart for God by opening your heart and mind.
5. Desire what He desires and your prayers will reflect His will.
6. Worship God with an undivided heart, focused on Him.

7. Remember that, "Blessed is the man whom God corrects; so do not despise the discipline of the Almighty," (Job 5:17). Let Him correct you in all areas of your life.
8. Take no action without first seeking God's wisdom.
9. Keep this Psalm of David in your heart at all times:

Then I acknowledged my sin to You and did not cover up my iniquity. I said, 'I will confess my transgressions to the Lord'" (Psalm 32:5).

10. Acknowledge God's presence every minute of every day, whether you need Him at that time or not. Remember that He is always near! You come close to Him, He will come close to you.
11. Plan a designated time for your meditation and communication with the Lord. Morning may be a good time for you: "In the morning, O Lord, you hear my voice; in the morning I lay my requests before you and wait in expectation (Psalm 5:3).
12. Remind yourself that all things can become good, no matter how bad they are. Psalm 119:71 will help you remember this concept, "It was good for me to be afflicted so that I might learn Your decrees."
13. Always adhere to this verse: "He has showed you, O man, what is good. And what does the Lord require of you? To act justly and to love mercy and to walk humbly with your God"(Micah 6:8).
14. Do not be afraid. Trust in Jesus. Reread this scripture frequently, "You came near when I called You, and You said, 'Do not fear'" (Lamentations 3:57).
15. Praise the Lord every day, "My heart is steadfast, O God; I will sing and make music with all my soul" (Psalm 108:1).
16. Reorder your day to ensure time for your communication with Jesus.

> *"Teach me Your way, O Lord, and I will walk in Your truth; give me an undivided heart, that I may fear Your name."* *(Psalm 86:11)*

CHAPTER 20

The Heart of the Matter... Focusing on the Will of God

"I trust in God's unfailing love for ever and ever.
I will praise You forever for what you have done;
in Your name I will hope, for Your name is good.
(Psalm 52:8-9)

Conclusion

As a result of a real heart attack, my heart was changed in an astounding way—changes you might find unbelievable. At my age and at my stage in life, I am as happy as I have ever been. I do not let disappointments, frustrations and lack of success in any aspect of my life bring me down. I know that what I focus on will affect my heart. My focus will also be manifested in my life: If all I think about is stress and fear, stress and fear will be manifested in my daily life; if I think about love and understanding and continue to follow God's will, love and understanding will be manifested in my life and I will receive God's promises.

I know that God wants me to continue to worship Him and serve Him in the ways that He has demonstrated to me. He has given me a second chance, a second chance to live and a second chance to live in His will. I will not waste the moments that remain in my life. I read this statement in Billy Graham's book, <u>Hope for Each Day</u>, in the message "Live for the Lord." He gives us all a "wake-up call": "Life passes so quickly it is almost over before we realize it—it is a snap of the finger compared to eternity. We have only a few brief years at the most. Let's live them for the Lord." This statement is a summary of my commitment: from this day on, I will live for the Lord!

There are already changes in all areas of my life and these changes are continuing to become more and more permanent every day. My work habits, time with my family, commitments to serve the Lord and finding time for increasing my personal relationship with Jesus have changed so that I may follow His will and His will can live in me in all environments, whether I am alone with the Lord or with people I need to serve and lead to Him. Pain caused these improvements in my life—is that not awesome? This quote from I Peter 2:19 gives me confidence that I am moving in the right direction according to God's will, "For it is commendable if a man bears up under the pain of unjust suffering because he is conscious of God." I was conscious of God before my heart attack. I prayed every day, almost every other minute of the day. But now, in prayer, I am listening to our Lord and I am conscious of His desires for me.

My services and my commitments will be made according to God's will, not my will. I am getting old and I am sometimes tired, but I feel renewed and revived. I know that I can continue to fulfill His plan for me and that He will fulfill His promises to me. I will refer to this scripture as I continue to live my life in Him, "Even youths grow tired and weary, and young men stumble and fall; but those who hope in the Lord will renew their strength. They will soar on wings like eagles; they will run and not grow weary, they will walk and not be faint" (Isaiah 40:30-31).

I thank the Lord God Almighty every day for saving my life and continuing to use me. I did request to be removed from this earth and join Him in heaven but the changes in my lifestyle have greatly affected my relationship with Jesus in a most positive way. I hope that my story will affect others and help them search their hearts as soon as possible. I feel that God has a mission for me to share this story with others and I am at peace with His decision. In

Romans 5:1-4, we read a perfect story about peace and joy and God's movement in our lives:

> *"Therefore, since we have been justified through faith, we have peace with God through our Lord Jesus Christ, through whom we have gained access by faith into this grace in which we now stand. And we rejoice in the hope of the glory of God. Not only so, but we also rejoice in our sufferings, because we know that suffering produces perseverance; perseverance, character; and character, hope.*

Our faith saves us. Jesus' blood washes away our sins. I know that I will try as hard as I can to live out His will in me. I will listen to His word and follow His lead in all areas of my life. I will pray to our Father to hear my needs but I will say what Jesus said, "Your will, not my will." I really believe this scripture as stated in Matthew 17:20, "I tell you the truth, if you have faith as small as a mustard seed, you can say to this mountain, 'Move from here to there,' and it will move. Nothing will be impossible for you."

I will always follow Jesus' directions in John 16:24, "Until now you have not asked for anything in my name. Ask and you will receive and your joy will be complete." Everything that I ask will always be in His name, according to His will. I will pray for all the needs that I see on earth and trust in our God to care for us and bless us. I want to reach out to others and bring them to Him. Jesus stated in John 20:21, "As the father has sent me, I am sending you."

"I will praise You, O Lord my God, with all my heart; I will glorify Your name forever. For great is Your love toward me." (Psalm 86:12)

www.ingramcontent.com/pod-product-compliance
Lightning Source LLC
LaVergne TN
LVHW011730060526
838200LV00051B/3101